Dickens

New Readings

Dickens

Kate Flint

Fellow and Tutor in English
Mansfield College, Oxford

HUMANITIES PRESS INTERNATIONAL, INC.
Atlantic Highlands, NJ

First published in 1986 in the United States of America by
HUMANITIES PRESS INTERNATIONAL, INC.,
Atlantic Highlands, NJ 07716

Library of Congress Cataloging-in-Publication Data

Flint, Kate.
  Dickens.

  (Harvester new readings)
  Bibliography: p.
  Includes index.
  1. Dickens, Charles, 1812–1870—Criticism and inter-
pretation.   I. Title.   II. Series.
PR4588.F55   1986   823′.8   86–320
ISBN 0–391–03419–7

PRINTED IN GREAT BRITAIN

For
Dorothy Bednarowska

Harvester New Readings

This major new series offers a range of important new critical introductions to English writers, responsive to new bearings which have recently emerged in literary analysis. Its aim is to make more widely current and available the perspectives of contemporary literary theory, by applying these to a selection of the most widely read and studied English authors.

The range of issues covered varies with each author under survey. The series as a whole resists the adoption of general theoretical principles, in favour of the candid and original application of the critical and theoretical models found most appropriate to the survey of each individual author. The series resists the representation of any single either traditionally or radically dominant discourse, working rather with the complex of issues which emerge from a close and widely informed reading of the author in question in his or her social, political and historical context.

The perspectives offered by these lucid and accessible introductory books should be invaluable to students seeking an understanding of the full range and complexity of the concerns of key canonical writers. The major concerns of each author are critically examined and sympathetically and lucidly reassessed, providing indispensable handbooks to the work of major English authors seen from new perspectives.

David Aers	*Chaucer*
Drummond Bone	*Byron*
Angus Calder	*T.S. Eliot*
Simon Dentith	*George Eliot*
Kelvin Everest	*Keats*
Kate Flint	*Dickens*
Paul Hamilton	*Wordsworth*
Brean Hammond	*Pope*
Kiernan Ryan	*Shakespeare*
Simon Shepherd	*Spenser*
Nigel Wood	*Swift*

Contents

Abbreviations

AN: *American Notes*
BH: *Bleak House*
BR: *Barnaby Rudge*
DC: *David Copperfield*
DS: *Dombey and Son*
ED: *The Mystery of Edwin Drood*
GE: *Great Expectations*
HT: *Hard Times*
LD: *Little Dorrit*
MC: *Martin Chuzzlewit*
NN: *Nicholas Nickleby*
OCS: *The Old Curiosity Shop*
OMF: *Our Mutual Friend*
OT: *Oliver Twist*
PP: *The Pickwick Papers*
SB: *Sketches by Boz*
TTC: *A Tale of Two Cities*
UT: *The Uncommercial Traveller*

References are to title and chapter; where page references are given too (in the case of *Sketches by Boz* and *The Uncommercial Traveller*), they are to the *New Oxford Illustrated Dickens*.

Acknowledgements

First of all, my thanks must go to those who have read and commented on all or part of this book during the course of its preparation: Joy Flint, Stephen Gill, Brean Hammond, Alastair Minnis, Rick Rylance and Dennis Walder. Any errors or infelicities are, of course, my own. Students in the English Department of Bristol University have helped me to try out my views, and have offered useful and stimulating ideas. I am also most grateful to Kelvin Everest, to Sue Roe of the Harvester Press, and to Jan Tarling and Marjorie Taylor, secretaries to the Department of English at Bristol, for their variegated brands of support and tolerance. In particular, I owe a considerable debt to the dedicatee, who first made me think seriously about Dickens.

Introduction

It is easy enough to enjoy reading Dickens; it is far less easy to try to write about his novels. The books fit neatly into no genres. Their plots are intriguingly complex but, by the end of the book, they seem to have evaporated in importance, leaving us thinking about the whole range of emotions and sensations which have been generated. Attempts to analyse Dickens' novels in terms of psychological realism are, in most cases, irrelevant or inadequate. The world described is both familiar to us in many of its attitudes, and distanced from us, through the different social forms, the slightly altered language, in which such attitudes are manifested. Pinning down exactly what it *is* that we find enjoyable can be harder still—the frequent changes of tone and style? the crowded descriptions? the unpredictable humorous incongruities? the viciousness of Dickens' attacks on the complacent and the hypocritical?

None of these aspects is hard to spot. What is difficult is to know what use to make of them. This study offers what may be called strategies of reading. Such strategies are not intended to explain Dickens' work, to answer and to tie up neatly the problems which it poses, but are to help recognise some of the premises on which it is based, to point to some of its affinities with the time at which it was written—from the point of view of organisation as well as of content—and to describe some of the effects which it has on us as readers. This strategic approach does not offer one exclusive mode of reading, but suggests ways of analysis which draw on many recent developments in structuralist, deconstructive, Marxist and feminist analysis. None the less, the book does not jettison the insights which may be offered by more traditional approaches. Not seeking a permanent abolition of the author, reasoned use is made of biographical material. In particular, the study acknowledges the enormous contribution made to Dickens studies by historical scholarship. Deliberately, aspects of these different critical approaches—the established and the new—are employed side by side, despite the contradictions and challenges which they pose, in an attempt to show that it is possible for them to be employed simultaneously. To take the approaches in labelled isolation, to provide, say, a 'structuralist' reading, followed by a 'feminist' one, followed by a 'psychoanalytic' one, would be to underplay the degree to which different critical methodologies have become dependent on one another, and would imply, falsely, that such critical templates can be placed over texts and readings neatly extracted from them.

To offer these various strategies of reading is to challenge not just some of the more old-fashioned assumptions made by writers on Dickens, but to call into question what may be some of our habits in reading and analysing much fiction. For this reason, I do not consider the novels one by one, but take my examples from wherever seems appropriate when looking at narrative point of view, or the discussion of social change, or the structuring of gender. I wish to stress the implications for fictionality in general, as well as to examine Dickens' methods of composition in particular. In a study of this length, to treat the novels singly would tempt one towards reductionism. But such an unchronological approach, reading across the board, is not intended to diminish the importance of history when approaching Dickens' fiction. Indeed, it is crucial that we recognise the distances and similarities between his time, his use of language, and our own.

To point to the various ways in which Dickens' fiction may be read is of little purpose, however, unless we have some clear idea of what we are doing it for. Why not just succumb to the escapist pleasures the novels offer? Three desirable ends above all can, I think, be put forward.

First, studying Dickens' writing enable us to recognise some of the techniques by which these pleasures are stimulated: variety, surprise and narrative complexity. This complexity is, on the surface, resolved by the final page, allowing us to share in a sense of completion, but it allows so many issues to escape from its tightly-drawn net during the course of the novel that we still remain in possession of a great deal of interpretative freedom—despite the occasional didactic passages which direct our reponse during the course of the novel. This interpretative responsibility can be turned back to consider the society about which Dickens was writing in order to feed the second of our ends: understanding the relationship between our time, and our ideological beliefs, and the past. For although this Victorian society is far enough removed from our own time to have acquired an allure, a patina of difference, it is, none the less, the period in which many of our current institutions and social formations first found full expression. Dickens, among other things, lays bare some of the means by which power was silently wielded in England, and the understanding which he offers, explicitly and implicitly, of how authority can be maintained, how beliefs become established and propagated, need not necessarily be limited to his own age.

3

Thirdly, the complexities of Dickens' writing, the variety of tones and points of view which it presents, are valuable to us in a way which combines the stylistically formal with the social. They remind us of the inherent impossibility of language, itself the shifting product and determinant of many historical and social forces, ever being able to mirror with any precision the society of its moment of inscription. The fact that there are no truths, only ways of seeing, is a proposition which it is well to bear in mind when tackling any literary work, and it is admirably exemplified by a careful reading of Dickens' novels themselves.

1

Dickens and an Age of Visible Transition

Dickens' writing is full of contradictions. It defies easy categorisation: he is both instructor and entertainer, social critic and practised humorist. He expresses deep pessimism about the future of his country and the stifling effects of the institutions which attempt to organise and structure it, yet, on the other hand, he is the optimist who wishes to stress that even the most stony heart is capable of regeneration. Such contradictions run through a huge body of texts: his fifteen novels, the Christmas Books, short stories, travel writings, the journalistic items collected in *Sketches by Boz* and the *Uncommercial Traveller*, pieces appearing in the periodicals which he edited—*Bentley's Miscellany*, the *Daily News*, *Household Words* and *All the Year Round*—and other articles, plays, poems, speeches and letters.

Reading Dickens now, in the 1980s, special difficulties face us. Whereas the original consumers received the novels in weekly or monthly parts, we are confronted with what perhaps seems a dauntingly fat volume, filled with vast hordes of characters, densely detailed descriptions and, particularly in the later works, plots of apparently tortuous complexity. Like the first readers, we find that Dickens' tone and point of view are continually changing—not so much from one novel to another, but within each novel. The satiric is juxtaposed with the coyly sentimental; the censorious with the frivolous. Minute observation alternates with social and psychological generalisation. Despite—even because of—our conscious enjoyment of this constant change, it is hard to settle into any one mode of reading.

Of course, it is not just our novel reading habits which differ from those of the Victorians. Dickens was an intensely contemporary writer, continually alluding to current social conditions and problems, whether slum housing or the railway mania, Yorkshire schools or London dust heaps. He drew on cultural frames of reference familiar to his readers: popular theatres and evangelical chapels, topical jokes and issues which had just been reported in the newspapers. For his readership, the society about which Dickens wrote was their own society, even if some of his novels were ostensibly set in a slightly earlier time. For us, despite the apparent familiarity of some of its aspects, it is a society about which we have to learn, about which we must be careful not to generalise too easily.

Many critics have attempted to account for the themes, the preoccupations, and the contradictions of Dickens' work by referring to incidents in his own life, or to what they surmise or deduce about his psychological make-up. Yet the game of 'hunt-the-author', however tempting, can be a misleading one, a desperate search for a stable, god-like source of authoritative meaning. Increasingly, under the influence of formalist, structuralist and post-structuralist critics, it has been argued that the business of criticism is not to find a key to what an author was 'trying' to say. (Why should we, the reader, think that we have the authority to see and speak clearly where he or she did not?) Rather than focusing on the author as the ultimate source of meaning and end-point of analysis, criticism has become increasingly concerned with exploring the existence and potentialities of what is there on a page: not with hypothesising about there being an original, pre-verbal meaning which has become obfuscated with its translation into words.

The object of studying Dickens' works, therefore, is certainly *not* to discover what he 'really' thought about anything. A knowledge of his life and circumstances, like those of any writer, provides us with no magic formula to guide us as to how his work may reliably be read. This fact becomes even more obvious when we consider how partial one's access to a dead literary figure is. It comes almost entirely through the inevitably slippery, unreliable medium of written language, whether this originates from the pen of the person concerned or takes the form of the reminiscences and records of others. Moreover, when we are dealing with what seem like manifestations of Dickens' 'real' voice—in letters, articles, and so on—these are, as we shall see, as much 'texts' as are his novels, and should be treated with the same guardedness. They represent what Dickens, consciously or unconsciously, wished to convey about himself at specific moments, and any claims which are made for their value on apparently objective grounds must be treated with the utmost caution.

None the less, if the details of Dickens' biography are in no way to be regarded as an unequivocal source of meaning, this certainly does not mean that we should ignore them. It is impossible to reach an adequate understanding of Dickens' novels without placing him within the context of the time in which he was writing: something which the greater part of this chapter will attempt to do.

To attempt to outline Dickens' full life here would lead, inevitably, to distorted potting; and the reader is referred to the brief chronology (pp. 142–4) and, more particularly, to section A of the Select Bibliography (pp. 145–7). One work in this area stands out as essential reading though: John Forster's *Life of Dickens* (1872–74); J.W. Ley's 1928 edition has admirably full explanatory notes. This is a unique document. It is the only Dickens biography written by someone who was not only a contemporary and close friend, but with whom the writer discussed incidents in his life which he disclosed to no one else. From a wider perspective, it is worth noting that Forster's literary preferences differed little from those of other middle-class readers of fiction, hence many of his comments and responses help indicate how Dickens' works were received by a substantial number of his contemporaries.

Two important generalisations emerge from Forster's biography which are of immediate relevance to us. First, Forster is especially emphatic about Dickens' strong belief that his personal past exercised an ineradicable influence not just on his personality, but on his writing. Pip, the first-person narrator of *Great Expectations*, utters a request at the end of Chapter 9: 'Pause you who read this, and think for a moment of the long chain of iron or gold, of thorns or flowers, that would never have bound you, but for the formation of the first link on one memorable day.' There is an uncomfortable suggestion here of being manacled to one's past just as the convicts were shackled to the hulks in the Thames estuary. The past can be a tyrant as well as a stimulus to enjoyable nostalgia. When Dickens told Forster, apropos of *David Copperfield*, that it was in part a dramatisation of his own life, he also remarked, 'I know how all those things have worked together to make me what I am.'[1] Whilst the novel should not be read primarily in a biographical light, its content does serve to remind us of his early apprenticeship as a writer. Like David, Dickens taught himself shorthand, recording the proceedings of Doctors' Commons, the setting of David's employment at Spenlow and Jorkins. Then, like his hero, he passed on to report parliamentary speeches, an experience which exposed him to a variety of matters of public concern, to numerous tricks and effects of rhetoric, and which gave him a lifelong dislike of Parliament and, *en masse*, of its members. Both the fictional David and the young Dickens submitted articles to newspapers; both, young, became successful novelists. When David remarks that he went 'to work with a resolute and steady heart' (DC: 36), that he 'truly devoted myself to [my writing] with my strong earnestness, and bestowed upon it every energy of my soul', Dickens seems to be reiterating a formula which had worked for himself, and which, for that matter, describes what is lacking in the aimless attempts of Richard Carstone in *Bleak House*, or Edward Dorrit, to take up careers. The almost obsessive diligence with which Dickens applied himself to the variety of literary and social tasks which he held simultaneously in hand would have provided a splendid biographical exemplar for that Victorian chronicler and exhorter of self-help, Samuel Smiles.

If there was a particular link in the chain of Dickens' life to which his imagination continually returned, it was his brief spell, as a twelve-year-old, in a blacking factory, made necessary by his family's increasingly desperate financial situation, and coinciding with his father's imprisonment for debt in the Marshalsea prison. Many critics have chosen to use this experience as the source for the prevalence in the novels of isolated, alienated individuals, deprived, for the most part, of secure parental affection. Sometimes, like Arthur Clennam or Sidney Carton, these are adults, more frequently, they are children: Oliver, Pip, Florence Dombey and, of course, David Copperfield. Indeed, the 'autobiographical fragment' in which Dickens recalls this time is almost identical to David's narration of his experience in Murdstone and Grinby's warehouse:

That I suffered in secret, and that I suffered exquisitely, no one ever knew but I. How much I suffered, it is, as I have said already, utterly beyond my power to tell. *No man's imagination can overstep the reality*. But I kept my own counsel, and I did my work. (DC: 11)[2]

Although otherwise this passage, and much more besides, is used verbatim, the sentence which I have emphasised does not appear in the novel. It is as though Dickens wished to stress that, for once, he has dropped his perennial habit of inventiveness and embroidery, common to his fiction and non-fiction alike. For all his reliance on the valuable faculty of imagination, this is the one topic on which it is fruitless, as well as dishonest, to bring it into play.

But, as F.S. Schwarzbach has pointed out, this experience, however deeply felt, was in fact presented by Dickens in a manner which owes more to myth-making than to strict accuracy. The vocabulary of his account for Forster plays on the traditional city-country antitheses: 'sunshine', 'bright' and 'wonderful romance' (despite the fact that Chatham, the town from which the Dickens family had come, was a bustling naval town, not a pastoral retreat) contrast with 'wretched' and 'squalid'. Moreover, he is vague about timings, suggesting that the period at Warren's began shortly after his arrival in the metropolis, when a period of thirteen months intervened, guessing at a year for the time he spent there, when it was probably four months, certainly no more than five. In other words, claims Schwarzbach, here is the man, the successful author, 'looking back at the helpless and impoverished child. It is not ... a literal account but is in certain respects a fabrication, or, if that sounds too extreme, an imaginative reconstruction, of his childhood.'[3] Such investigations demonstrate clearly how searching for explanations in autobiographical evidence must, at best, be an uncertain exercise. But it does nothing to minimise the shock of dislocation felt by Dickens at his experience: a shock not merely experienced at a personal, familial level, but one which highlighted the precariousness of class position.

It could well be argued that this adolescent experience fed into the second important point that we can take from Forster's biography: the fact that, throughout his life, Dickens deliberately developed a cult of personality: 'Undoubtedly one of the impressions [he leaves] is that of the intensity and tenacity with which he recognized, realized, contemplated, cultivated and thoroughly enjoyed, his own individuality in even its most trivial manifestations'.[4] This sense of self-dramatisation permeates Dickens' non-fictional writings, whether his journalism or his letters, where we see him turning each trivial incident of family life, or travelling in France or Italy, into a minute playlet with himself at the centre. Their habitual tone of slightly self-mocking irony does little to diminish the unashamed egocentricity with which the starring persona constructs himself. This projection of self is found in Dickens' speeches, too. Above all, he traded on this image of an energetic, unfragmented ego when it came to the public readings of the last years of his life; he used it, in fact, to sustain him in the face of private difficulties. In other words, when the Victorian public responded to 'Dickens', they were reacting to more than the effect of the words on the page which it is possible to describe by the use of his name. They were reacting to a conscious projection of personality. This closeness to his readers was something which Dickens relished, and something which his particular mode of publication played upon. The appearance of his novels in serial form had advantages for Dickens as publisher. It enabled a high circulation, allowing him to spread his costs (which could be minimised through receipts from advertisers), and it assured him independence from the demands of the powerful circulating libraries which sought, to some extent, to control both the length and the content of novels published in volume form. Additionally, publication in parts meant that readers could act as collaborators in the production of the novels. Dickens paid great attention to audience response, whether expressed directly through correspondence or conversation or, more obliquely, through circulation figures. Although when the publication of a novel began, he normally had some four or five numbers ready, by the middle of a work he was unlikely to be more than one number ahead. Thus, even with his first full-length work, *Pickwick Papers* (1836–37), they could prompt the development of Sam Weller 'to the utmost';[5] while Martin Chuzzlewit was sent off to the United States in an attempt to revive declining sales figures. In the case of *Dombey and Son* (1846–48), letters from readers influenced Dickens against showing Walter Gay 'gradually and naturally trailing away, from that love of adventure and boyish light-heartedness, into negligence, idleness, dissipation, dishonesty and ruin ... to show how the good turns into bad, by degrees.'[6] In the same novel, public pressure prevented Edith Dombey from succumbing to Carker's sexual ambitions and, tantalisingly, deprived Dickens of giving us a projected scene of Carker sinking his gleaming teeth into Edith's breast.[7] We may legitimately speak of ourselves as producers of meaning as we read Dickens' novels—deriving our understanding from their words in proportion to our own linguistic, literary and historical competence—but these original readers became co-producers in a concrete, material sense, their demands altering the course of events and the presentation of protagonists.

Dickens may have encouraged his contemporaries to see him in this dual light: as one who was both a larger-than-life individual, and as one who was so close to their tastes and sentiments that he could merge his voice with theirs. It can help us, when placing him in his time, to put aside for the time being the claims of uniqueness which he implicitly made for himself, and which have subsequently been made countless times for him, and to consider him from the opposite point of view, as one among many.

London is at the centre of much of Dickens' writing, and his novels betray an ambivalence of emotions towards it. Overcrowded, full of disease and cime, it is a site of problems from which Dickens eventually liberates certain favoured characters, such as Oliver Twist and Esther Summerson. Yet others, particularly Clennam and Amy Dorrit, will, it is suggested, draw strength from a projected future in the city's busy, beating heart. However much the writing might overtly deplore the conditions of urban life, it would be hard to deny that some of Dickens' tautest, most original, most energetic prose has its origins in such descriptions. His own pronouncements on the subject of the metropolis in a letter to Bulwer Lytton were similarly ambivalent:

London is a vile place, I sincerely believe. I have never taken kindly to it, since I lived abroad. Whenever I come back from the country now, and see that great heavy canopy lowering over the housetops, I wonder what on earth I do there except on obligation.[8]

But evidently, when away from the city, he also claimed to pine for its stimulating diversity. When in Genoa, in 1844, he wrote: 'Put me down on Waterloo Bridge at eight o'clock in the evening, with leave to roam about as long as I like, and I would come home, as you know, panting to go on.[9] As his daughter Kate recalled, when Dickens was working on a novel, 'he would walk through the busy, noisy streets, which would act on him like a tonic and enable him to take up with new vigour the flagging interest of his story and breathe new life into its pages.'[10]

Yet Dickens was not a native Londoner. His family only moved there from Chatham, Kent, when he was ten years old.

They were not the capital's only new inhabitants. The city grew vastly during his lifetime: in 1801, the capital had 1,088,000 inhabitants; by 1851, 2,491,000. And this growth was slow compared with other, provincial cities. Between 1801 and 1851, the ratio of country to urban population shifted from 70:30 to 49:51. Edward Bulwer Lytton, in *England and the English* (1833), remarked aptly that 'Every age may be called an age of transition—the passing on . . . from one state to another never ceases; but in our age the transition is *visible*.'[11] Nowhere is this more apparent than in the rapid, shoddy and speculatory expansion of London which Dickens describes. In *The Old Curiosity Shop*, Nell and her grandfather pass 'damp rotten houses, many to let, many yet building, many half-built and mouldering away' (OCS: 15); in *Dombey and Son*, cataclysmic upheaval to already existing homes and to the environment is brought by the northern advance of the railway. When Susan, Florence and Paul go to visit Paul's former nurse in Staggs's Gardens:

> The first shock of a great earthquake had, just at that period, rent the whole neighbourhood to its centre . . . Everywhere were bridges that led nowhere; thoroughfares that were wholly impassable; Babel towers of chimneys, wanting half their height . . . Hot springs and fiery eruptions, the usual attendants upon earthquakes, lent their contributions of confusion to the scene. (DS: 6)

The results of this conspicuous process of change are visible six years later. When Walter searches out the Toodles, he finds that:

> There was no such place as Staggs's Gardens . . . The old by-streets now swarmed with passengers and vehicles of every kind: the new streets that had stopped disheartened in the mud and waggon-ruts, formed towns within themselves . . . Bridges that

had led to nothing, led to villas, gardens, churches, healthy public walks. (DS: 15)

And the city is still pushing outwards, leaping over tracts of 'suburban Sahara', when Dickens describes the landscape in *Our Mutual Friend*.

The vastness of the city, the sense of anonymity created both by its size, and by the number of people it contained, produced a sense of alienation which, by the time that Dickens was writing, was already something of a literary commonplace. Wordsworth described it in Book 7 of *The Prelude*, where the 'perpetual flow' of the 'mighty city' is a 'blank confusion'; where

> often in the overflowing streets
> Have I gone forwards with the crowd, and said
> Unto myself, 'The face of every one
> That passes by me is a mystery.'[12]

But the fact that the association of the image of the city with frightening experience had, to a certain extent, become formalised did not eliminate the experience of alienation. Engels noted in *The Condition of the Working Class in England* (1844) that

A town such as London, where a man might wander for hours together without reaching the beginning of the end, without meeting the slightest hint which could lead to the inference that there is open country within reach, is a strange thing. This colossal centralisation, this heaping together of two and a half millions of human beings at one point, has multiplied the power of this two and a half millions a hundredfold ... The hundreds of thousands of all classes and ranks crowding past each other, are they not all human beings with the same qualities and powers, and with the same interest in being happy? ... And still they crowd by one another as though they had nothing in common,

15

nothing to do with one another, and their only agreement is the tacit one, that each keep to his own side of the pavement, so as not to delay the opposing stream of the crowd, while it occurs to no man to honour another with so much as a glance. The brutal indifference, the unfeeling isolation of each in his private interest, becomes the more repellent and offensive, the more these individuals are crowded together, within a limited space.[13]

Dickens himself, of course, alludes to the indifference of contemporary city life. In *Sketches by Boz*, for example, he notes that 'it is strange with how little notice, good, bad, or indifferent, a man may live and die in London' (SB: p. 215); and in *The Old Curiosity Shop*, he refers to those 'who live solitary in great cities as in the bucket of a human well' (OCS: 15). London sucks people into its anonymity. In *Dombey and Son*, Harriet Carker looks out on 'a stream of life setting that way, and flowing, indifferently' down the road towards the metropolis (DS: 33). It is this combination of anonymity and centripetal force which makes the city such a useful narrative tool: a source, in its multitudinity, of all kinds of fictional types; a probable converging place for established characters. It is both the healthy heart of the nation, receiving the trains which hurtle into the railway terminus past the site of Staggs's Gardens—'all day and night, throbbing currents rushed and returned incessantly like its life's blood' (DS: 15)—and, simultaneously, the source of the disease which enfeebles the body politic. In *Our Mutual Friend*, 'the whole metropolis' is seen as 'a heap of vapour charged with muffled sounds of wheels, and enfolding a gigantic catarrh' (OMF: III, 1). Chapters 3 and 4 will elaborate on some of the narrative and interpretative strategies employed by Dickens in his attempt to subdue and control the sense of alienation, produced not just by the vastness of the city, but by the social and economic forms which structured Victorian urban, capitalist society. Within this society, as Dickens was deeply aware, the individual rapidly became enmeshed, if not submerged, in large, unwieldy, but extraordinarily powerful systems.

One must not read Dickens, however, expecting to find any extractable, unificatory overview of this society. For, as he demonstrates both consciously and unwittingly in his novels, he was writing about, and for, a society deeply divided by two major factors: class and gender. It was a society which looked, and looks, very different when viewed from different angles. The distinction made by Disraeli in his novel *Sybil* (1845) between 'two nations: THE RICH AND THE POOR'[14] became, in its stark absoluteness, almost a catch-phrase of mid-nineteenth-century concern. At times, Dickens too presented the city's irreconcilable contradictions as neat antitheses, very much according to a satiric tradition consolidated in eighteenth-century writing. Thus, for example, when Nicholas Nickleby arrives in London with Smike:

The rags of the squalid ballad-singer fluttered in the rich light that showed the goldsmith's treasures, pale and pinched-up faces hovered about the windows where was tempting food, hungry eyes wandered over the profusion guarded by the thin sheet of brittle glass—an iron wall to them; half-naked shivering figures stopped to gaze at Chinese shawls and golden stuffs of India. There was a christening party at the largest coffin-maker's, and a funeral hatchment had stopped some great improvements in the bravest mansion. Life and death went hand in hand; wealth and poverty stood side by side; repletion and starvation laid them down together. (NN: 32)

But such set-pieces of formally organised writing are relatively rare, particularly in the later novels. In general, Dickens' fiction, whilst never ignoring the polarities of the slums of St Giles, and fashionable St James's, reminds us that he was writing within a period when the social balance was not at all as static as such a crude dichotomy would suggest: where the ironmaster could become as powerful as the aristocrat had been; where upward mobility was possible— Pip, in *Great Expectations*, enacts the process of becoming a gentleman in terms of a contemporary moral fable. Possible, too, were sudden reversals of financial fortune, especially with the vicissitudes of investment and speculation within a cash-based economy. We see this above all with the speculative rise and subsequent collapse of Merdle's finances in *Little Dorrit*. Dickens' novels are sensitive to the grey conditions of shabby respectability: the immense difference, on an annual income of twenty pounds, between an expenditure of nineteen pounds nineteen and six, and twenty pounds aught and six.

We shall return to the question of class later, and in particular to the paradox that whilst Dickens was intensely angry at appalling social conditions, his vituperative attacks on those with judicial and administrative responsibility were coupled with an apparent resistance to the idea of any substantial alteration to the class structure. Here, however, we may briefly consider it in relation to the original consumers of his works. There is considerable evidence that the readership of Dickens' novels, especially the earlier ones, crossed class boundaries. We have both the reactions of the aristocracy—Lord Melbourne said of *Oliver Twist* that 'It is all among workhouses and pickpockets and coffinmakers. I do not like them in reality and therefore do not like to see them represented'[15]—and the testimony of the *National Magazine*:

> Even the common people, both in town and country, are equally intense in their admiration. Frequently we have seen the butcher-boy, with his tray on his shoulder, reading with the greatest avidity the last 'Pickwick'; the footman (whose fopperies are so intimately laid bare), the maidservant, the chimney-sweep, all classes, in fact, read 'Boz'.[16]

Dickens' huge contemporary popularity certainly cannot be doubted: the sale in monthly parts of his novels averaged about 40,000 copies, and the demand did not appear to slacken with his death. In 1882 it was reported that in England alone, the sale of his work in the twelve years since his death amounted to some 4,239,000 volumes.[17] However, as George H. Ford reminds us in *Dickens and his Readers*, we must be cautious here, as elsewhere, about generalisations. It is hard to find evidence below a certain social and economic level of readership of any kind because of the paucity of such extant sources as diaries and letters. Morever, in 1850, 8 million people in England and Wales—almost a quarter of the population—could neither read nor write. It is safer to suggest that the majority of Dickens' readers belonged to what in general terms can be described as the middle classes, and most of his working-class audience belonged to the skilled sector: the type he addressed in mechanics' institutes in Birmingham, Manchester and Coventry, where he heard explicit thanks for the fact that in his work there was not

> a single word that tended to irritate one class of society against another; but, on the contrary, his writings have tended to bind them together with the common sentiments of humanity and common feelings of Christian love.[18]

The public voice of this audience, at any rate, was not willing to admit to the possiblity that his writings might be read in a way which would work towards emphasising, rather than narrowing, class differences.

Little evidence exists which suggests that responses to Dickens' works differed according to the gender of those reading them, despite the highly divergent views and expectations which were held throughout the period with respect to men and women. Only an occasional, usually male, voice is heard complaining that the stress which is placed in

the earlier volumes on alcoholic conviviality makes them
unsuitable for the delicate ear. The metaphor of family used
by Dickens to describe the relationship which he hoped to
hold with his audience militates, on the surface, against any
such gender-based differentiation in the novels' reception. It
suggests a homogeneity of responsible good feeling. Yet, on a
deeper level, it necessarily reinforces gender distinctions,
since, through consolidating the idea of a closely-knit family
group as a social norm, it reminds one of woman's symbolic
place at the hearthside, the focus of family reading, of
'household words'. It also reinforces the middle-class appeal
of Dickens' work: the class in which cultural values were
above all generated and transmitted in the home, as opposed
to the street or workplace.

Drawing attention to differences of gender and class among
readers, as well as among the variety of characters and types
portrayed in the novels, is one way of reminding ourselves of
the variety of perspectives and points of view which
constituted 'Victorian society'. The concept of unity is
shattered, too, when we recognise the process of rapid change
which was so noticeable during the period when Dickens was
writing: a recognition which commentators later in Victoria's
reign were fond of making. Walter Besant, writing at the time
of the Silver Jubilee in 1888, recalled 1837, the year of
Victoria's accession, and of the volume publication of
Pickwick. Then, he claimed, 'we were still, to all intents and
purposes, in the eighteenth century'. He outlined what had
been, for him, the most significant changes:

Rank was still held in the ancient reverence; religion was still that
of the eighteenth-century Church; the rights of labour were not
yet recognised; there were no trades' unions; there were no
railways to speak of; nobody travelled except the rich; their own
country was unknown to the people; the majority of country
people could not read or write; the good old discipline of Father

Stick and his children, Cat-o'-Nine-Tails, Rope's end, Strap, Birch, Ferule, and Cane, was wholesomely maintained; landlords, manufacturers, and employers of all kinds did what they pleased with their own.[19]

Besant, like many commentators towards the end of the century, laid great stress on the development of the railways, that quintessential image of progress for any retrospectively-inclined Victorian. Thackeray, writing in 1860, boldly juxtaposed images of fuedal and modern to highlight the extraordinary difference between the world into which he was born, and that in which he now lived; and then seized on the crucial factor: 'your railroad starts the new era, and we of a certain age belong to the new time and the old one.'[20] This is the 'triumphant monster' of *Dombey and Son*, the 'conquering engines', the 'tame dragons', about which Dickens writes with a mixture of fascinated admiration and horror.

The impact of the growing rail network—the first track, from Liverpool to Manchester, was laid in 1830; by 1850, there were 6621 miles—was enormous. It served and made possible the rapidly growing industrial centres, making easy the transport of raw materials and finished products. And not only was personal mobility facilitated; so, too, was the conveyance of newspapers, magazines and mail, including, of course, novels, whether in volume or part format, to the booksellers. Moreover, for the enthusiastic middle-class Victorian, the concept of drawing lines of communication and control over the map was not limited to this island. Dickens' lifetime saw the extension of British rule in India; the exploration of much of tropical Africa; the expansion of South Africa; the foundation of New Zealand, and the settlement and development of Australia, with the consequent increase in emigration. This country, as well as receiving criminals—the Artful Dodger in *Oliver Twist*, Magwitch in *Great Expectations*—provided a fictional destination, convenient in its probability, for such characters as the seduced but repentant Emily in *David Copperfield*, or the perpetually impecunious Micawbers. In *Dombey and Son*, Dickens conveys the sense of London's position at the commercial centre of empire. Just around the corner from the offices of Dombey

> stood the rich East India House, teeming with suggestions of precious stuffs and stones, tigers, elephants, howdahs, hookahs, umbrellas, palm trees, palanquins, and gorgeous princes of a brown complexion sitting on carpets, with their slippers very much turned up at the toes. Anywhere in the immediate vicinity there might be seen pictures of ships speeding away full sail to all parts of the world... (DS: 4)

This tone of expansionist, commercial pride finds countless echoes in the press of the time. But in his fiction in general, Dickens does not use colonialism to reinforce a favourable impression of contemporary England. From *Pickwick* onwards, he attacked the misdirected philanthropy it could encourage. Satirically, he presents in this novel the Rev. Mr Stiggins, getting up subscribers to provide the 'infant negroes of the West Indies with flannel waistcoats and moral pocket-handkerchiefs', an effort put in perspective by the unimpressed Tony Weller: 'wot aggravates me ... is to see 'em a wastin' all their time and labour in making clothes for copper-coloured people as don't want 'em, and taking no notice of flesh-coloured Christians as do' (PP: 27).

This protest occurs within the framework of Dickens' one novel where, despite the occasional disquieting, disrupting references to social hardship, the prevalent atmosphere is that which John Morley described as being characteristic of the ruling classes after the Reform Bill of 1832, as their attention turned 'from the letter of institutions to their spirit.... A great wave of humanity, of benevolence, of desire for improvement—a great wave of moral sentiment, in short—poured itself among all who had the faculty of large and disinterested thinking.[21] But this narrative stance did not last, having no more solid a foundation than did Morley's optimism. The first three instalments of *Oliver Twist* (which appeared in *Bentley's Miscellany*, at irregular intervals, between February 1837 and April 1839), with their scathing assaults on the conditions supposedly created by the new Poor Law of 1834, attacking those who practised repressive inhumanitarianism under the cloak of moral religious respectability and authority, confirmed Dickens as the critic of contemporary society, the meticulous yet idiosyncratic observer which his non-fictional writings had already shown him to be. So by *Bleak House*, his treatment of Mrs Jellyby, preoccupied with her Mission, 'cultivating coffee and educating the natives of Borrioboola-Gha, on the left bank of the Niger' (BH: 4) is not an isolated, if heartfelt gibe, but forms part of his composite picture of near-wilful blindness on the part of many at home to the condition of England. He had already forcibly expressed his opinions on this very subject in an article of 1848 when he spoke of the need for widening circles of social enlightenment to spread out from London, like ripples emanating from a stone

> dropped into the ocean of ignorance ... but no convulsive effort, or far-off aim, can make the last great outer circle first, and then come home at leisure to trace out the inner one. Believe it, African Civilisation, Church of England Missionary, and all other Missionary Societies! The work at home must be completed thoroughly, or there is no hope abroad.[22]

In other words, Dickens' novels and other writings give the lie to those many contemporaries who, with complacency, nostalgicly represented the first decades of Victoria's reign as a laudable period of progress. But Victorian self-congratulation was not just retrospective. Dickens' anger, and the direct appeals which he makes to his readers from the novels' narratives, were voiced against a contemporary background of self-applause.

In 1851, the year Dickens began writing *Bleak House* (published March 1852–September 1853), a huge building was erected in Hyde Park. Covering 18 acres, with 1¾ miles of exhibition galleries, the glass and iron Crystal Palace was, in its own right, intended as a testimony to the excellence of Victorian engineering. Inside could be seen the goods of some 15,000 exhibitors. The public crowded in to admire Nasmyth's steam-hammer, capable of striking a blow of 500 tons; hydraulic presses; steam mills; portable steam-engines; models of iron bridges; patent iron threshing-machines and seed drills—whilst at the other end of the halls could be seen furniture and statuary—everything from sideboards to electroplated candlesticks, copper baths to asparagus tongs: relatives of the caravan of camels which 'take charge of the fruits and flowers and candles, and kneel down to be loaded with salt' on the fashion-conscious Veneerings' dinner table (OMF: I, 2).

The writers of *The Crystal Palace, and its Contents; an Illustrated Cyclopædia of the Great Exhibition* emphasised the theme of national pride, speaking rhapsodically of

> the country of Wedgwood, of Arkwright, and of Watt—the seat of the most advanced manufacturing processes, the focus of unlimited capital, the spot where laden vessels radiate in every direction, the country whose flag floats above more wealth than any rival state can boast, whose scientific men have led the way in the pursuit of wealth, whose legislators have stood in the van of political progress. . .[23]

But, ten days after the Exhibition opened, at the first anniversary banquet of the Metropolitan Sanitary Association, held just up the road in Kensington, the Earl of Carlisle asked his hearers to reflect on a different aspect of the Crystal Palace. He admitted that it was

> itself a shrine of labour.... But, while we gaze on the large area of its vast extent, on the wondrous results of its harmonious and completed combinations ... let us not refrain from tracing them back to that crowded workshop, that damp cellar, and that stifling garret.[24]

The main speaker on this occasion was Dickens, putting forward his fervent demand for 'Searching Sanitary Reform [since] even Education and Religion can do nothing where they are most needed, until the way is paved for their ministrations by Cleanliness and Decency.' He reminded his audience that disease caused by appalling living conditions would not stay quietly in the East End, its place of origin. Thus, the problems of an area of London which the comfortably off preferred to ignore would force themselves on their attention. It is certain that

> the air from Gin Lane will be carried, when the wind is Easterly, into May Fair, and that if you once have a vigorous pestilence raging furiously in Saint Giles's, no mortal list of Lady Patronesses can keep it out of Almack's.[25]

The theme of social interconnectedness had already been raised with blatant explicitness in Dickens' fiction. In the 1841 introduction to *Oliver Twist*, he spoke in defence of using 'curious coincidences' which 'show how people are all connected, one with another, in surprising ways'. Drawing an analogy in *Dombey and Son* between the child-robber Mrs Brown and her ruined daughter Alice, and another mother and daughter from a different stratum of society, the narrator asks:

Were this miserable mother, and this miserable daughter, only the reduction to their lowest grade, of certain social vices sometimes prevailing higher up? In this round world of many circles within circles, do we make a journey from the high grade to the low, to find at last that they lie close together, that the two extremes touch, and that our journey's end is but our starting place? Allowing for great differences of stuff and texture, was the pattern of this woof repeated among gentle blood at all?

Say, Edith Dombey! And Cleopatra, best of mothers, let us have your testimony! (DS: 34)

In *Bleak House*, the point is reinforced once again, this time to make a far more overtly political suggestion about recognising the need to acknowledge social responsibility. The narrator asks rhetorically, 'What connection can there be' between the sumptuous town and country properties of the aristocracy, and 'Jo the outlaw with the broom', coming from the 'black, dilapidated street, avoided by all decent people', in the decaying tenement of Tom-All-Alone's (BH: 16).

The plot of *Bleak House*, with its convoluted coincidences, may seem to provide a rather artificial answer to this question. But it serves to illustrate the theme of the inexorable interdependence of parts which, for Dickens, underpinned society. Despite his belief that words could stimulate actions, or produce the change of heart from which such actions might spring, they must, for him, never function as a substitute for deeds. Hence he was bitter that the condition of the extreme poor, as exemplified by the inhabitants of Tom-All-Alone's, could be discussed, at a distance, by those in power without their accepting accountability and practical duty. Satirically, the narrative voice comments that 'there is but one thing perfectly clear, to wit, that Tom only may and can, or shall and will, be reclaimed according to somebody's theory but nobody's practice' (BH: 46). Particularly culpable were those who refused to admit that society was in a state of flux, such as those members of elegant society who gathered at Chesney Wold:

> For whom everything must be languid and pretty.... On whom even the Fine Arts, attending in powder and walking backward like the Lord Chamberlain must array themselves in the milliners' and tailors' patterns of past generations, and be particularly careful not to be in earnest, or to receive any impress from the moving age. (BH: 12).

The simile neatly links parliamentary ceremonial with the attitudes of some of its constituent members. It helps emphasise how Dickens, in the middle and later stages of his career, clearly saw blame resting with institutions, even if these institutions may find their concrete embodiment in individuals. Yet, paradoxically, without some enlightenment on the part of individuals, nothing, the novels suggest, will ever change.

Mid-nineteenth-century society might have been less conspicuously brutal than that of the eighteenth century, even though until 1868, for example, it still practised the public executions which so appalled Dickens. There was a far greater consciousness of social hardship; great efforts took place to effect reforms in sanitary and housing conditions. But it was a period, also, when the state conspicuously consolidated its authority over the individual. Dickens' texts exemplify the contradictions which John Ruskin remarked on in 1875:

> Believe me, in spite of our political liberality, and poetical philanthropy; in spite of our almshouses, hospitals, and Sunday schools; in spite of our missionary endeavours to preach abroad what we cannot get believed at home; and in spite of our wars against slavery, indemnified by the presentation of ingenious bills,—we shall be remembered in history as the most cruel, and therefore the most unwise, generation of men that yet troubled the earth:—the most cruel in proportion to their sensibility,—the

most unwise in proportion to their science. No people, understanding pain, ever inflicted so much: no people, understanding facts, ever acted on them so little.[26]

Dickens' writings can never be called radical in terms of any of the solutions at which he hinted in response to this confusion. But they do enable us to see something of the complex dynamic of interrelating power structures, the systems of ideas as well as such institutions as law, Parliament, schools and the Church, which constituted the processes which we can be tempted to sum up by the convenient, if glib term 'Victorian society'.

In writing about his society, Dickens, like any other author, was forced to select, to stress, to organise, to manipulate the medium of language. His contemporaries seemed perplexed by the apparent verisimilitude offered by his crammed descriptive passages, which contrasted with the obvious artificiality of his plots, with his fantastic use of metaphor—turning people into leaves of tables, like Twemlow in *Our Mutual Friend*; of synecdoche, allowing them to be known by their buttons or wooden leg alone; of anthropomorphisation, transforming chimney cowls into dowager ladies fluttering their petticoats, identifying houses with both the appearance and ideology of their inhabitants. 'So crowded is the canvas which Mr Dickens has stretched', commented the *Spectator*'s critic of *Bleak House*,

and so casual the connexion that gives to his composition whatever unity it has, that a daguerreotype of Fleet Street at noon-day would be the aptest symbol to be found for it; though the daguerreotype would have the advantage in accuracy of representation.[27]

Dickens can certainly not be called a 'realist' in the simple sense of the word, which seeks an equation between the written form and a photographically verisimilitudinal representation of the world. Despite his acute visual sense, his writing is not like the 'great looking-glass above the sideboard' which reflects the superficiality of the Veneerings' dinner party. The picture on the shiny surface of this mirror, in *Our Mutual Friend*, acts as a metaphor in itself, emphasising that indeed there is nothing interesting or worthwhile about the guests at this gathering: that there is nothing beneath their showy façade. But if Dickens holds a mirror up to his society, it is, one might say, a cracked one: one which produces playful distortions and exaggerations for the sake of social, moral and aesthetic effect. Morover, the very unevenness of the reflection reminds us that the society observed can be seen from a multitude of angles and points of view, and there may be aspects of society which escape direct reflection in the text—we must supply, by our reading and analysis, what is caught, as it were, in the cracks of the mirror. What is more, once one accepts that Dickens' mirror does not have a flat, reliable surface, one is driven to look beneath this surface, to look at the techniques which, consciously and unconsciously, Dickens used to structure the varied presentations of content within his fictions. First, however, let us consider more closely those unresolvable contradictions which permeate Dickens' writing. Recognising some of these contradictions may, simultaneously, lead us to see some of the means by which his novels may profitably, as well as enjoyably, be read.

2

The Starving Clown: Dickens and Contradiction

In *Pickwick Papers*, Dickens' first full-length fictional work, Mr Pickwick is introduced as the epitome of innocent bonhomie. Although he is the central figure in the work, 'The author's object', Dickens states in his preface to the 1837 edition, 'was to place before the reader a constant succession of characters and incidents.' He was following the eighteenth-century picaresque tradition in constructing his novel in this loose, episodic way, despite taming the bawdy sexuality of these earlier novels and keeping only, it would seem, the more publicly acceptable gratifications of unstinted eating and drinking. Even though the tone of the novel darkens somewhat after Pickwick's confinement in the Fleet prison, its energetic good humour has been commended from its earliest reviewers onwards. The fact that many of the jokes and much of the slapstick action have necessarily dated considerably seems, perhaps surprisingly, to have worried few critics.

One reason for this may be the fact that the novel is not irredeemably light-hearted. Despite Dickens' disingenuous disclaimer that, given the sprawling character of his narrative, 'no artfully interwoven or ingeniously complicated plot can with reason be expected' (PP: 1837 preface), the novel does in fact show a careful interweaving of interpolated tales (a technique which in its turn owes something to eighteenth-century practice) which throw into relief the often thoughtless cheerfulness of the main parts of the book.

As early as Chapter 3, Pickwick falls into conversation with his complete opposite, a careworn, gaunt, strolling player, who proceeds to relate the first of these sobering stories. This 'dismal individual' describes a pantomime actor of his acquaintance. Though he had been out of touch with him for over a year, one night, on leaving the theatre, he had felt a tap on the shoulder:

> Never shall I forget the repulsive sight that met my eyes when I turned round. He was dressed for the pantomime, in all the absurdity of a clown's costume. The spectral figures in the Dance of Death, the most frightful shapes that the ablest painter ever portrayed on canvas, never presented an appearance half so ghastly. His bloated body and shrunken legs—their deformity enhanced a hundredfold by the fantastic dress—the glassy eyes, contrasting fearfully with the thick white paint with which the face was besmeared; the grotesquely ornamented head, trembling with paralysis, and the long, skinny hand, rubbed with white chalk—all gave him a hideous and unnatural appearance, of which no description could convey an adequate idea, and which to this day I shudder to think of. His voice was hollow and tremulous, as he took me aside, and in broken words recounted a long catalogue of sickness and privations—terminating, as usual, with an urgent request for a loan of a trifling sum of money. I put a few shillings in his hand, and as I turned away I heard the roar of laughter which followed his first tumble on to the stage.(PP: 3)

Beneath the greasepaint lies poverty and disease. Dickens loved the popular theatre. In general, its presence in his fictions serves to dramatise one of his key aesthetic principles: the principle he shared with the showman Sleary in *Hard Times*, that 'people must be amuthed' (HT: I,7). An evening at Astley's circus followed by oysters and beer is likely, we see in *The Old Curiosity Shop*, to have a far more uplifting effect on the spirit than any amount of evangelical sermonising in the chapel of Little Bethel. But here he is suggesting that there is a time for stripping off layers of theatrical make-up to see what lies beneath.

The removal of masks is a recurrent practice in Dickens' texts. Sometimes it is done literally. In *Dombey and Son*, Mrs Skewton's maid releases the elderly lady from the captivating pose which she adopts during the day:

> The painted object shrivelled under her hand; the form collapsed, the hair dropped off, the arched dark eyebrows changed to scanty tufts of grey; the pale lips shrunk, the skin became cadaverous and loose; an old, worn, yellow, nodding woman, with red eyes, alone remained in Cleopatra's place, huddled up, like a slovenly bundle, in a greasy flannel gown. (DS: 27)

Extending the idea metaphorically, we can see that if the Veneerings, in *Our Mutual Friend*, were to be stripped of their shiny surface, some very shoddy social furniture would be found. Their very name, playing on contemporary associations with the pretensions to good taste in decor which were held by the vulgar *nouveaux riches*, tells the discriminating reader this without Dickens having to spell out the social point.

When the aesthetic surface is peeled away, Dickens is not usually content to take the first, and most obvious explanation for what he sees. A fervent teetotaller could, no doubt, attribute the starving clown's destitute state to the evils of alcoholism, and leave it at that. But the story in *Pickwick Papers* is used to point to no such easy moral; rather, it is left hanging in the air, without gloss. Only later in the novel, as these gloomy interpolations pile up, can we see that they provide the backcloth of various human and economic depressions against which Pickwick's own attitudes appear the more innocent and limited, hinting that even if he can afford to ignore, for the most part, the darker sides of society, the reader cannot. In relation to the problem of alcoholism again, we can find elsewhere a good example which demonstrates how Dickens believed that responsibility for hardship goes far beyond the temperamental failings of an individual. He attacked the temperance tracts of the illustrator, George Cruikshank—*The Bottle*, and *The Drunkard's Children*—for their assumption that poverty is caused by a weakness for drink alone. Rather, he considered it the duty of the moralist to 'strike deep', and see alcoholism as symptom rather than cause: symptom of poor housing, bad working conditions, inadequate sanitation and, above all, ignorance.[1] Attention must be paid, he insisted, to the wider context of social deprivation, not just to the specific evil.

Thus, as we shall see, the unmasking of disguises, the unpeeling of surfaces, extended, for Dickens, into the whole presentation of Victorian society, and hence to the conventions, the fictions by which its ruling classes attempted to control, order and explain it. The slow-grinding machinery of the legal system, particularly in the Chancery courts; the unimaginative, uninformed identikit politicians, such as Boodle, Coodle and Foodle; and the endless red tape, the referral of inquiries from one room of bored bureaucrats to another in the Circumlocution Office, are clear butts of Dickens' explicit antagonism towards certain methods of social control. All, in their current forms, were self-perpetuating, self-justifying mechanisms, peculiarly slow in thinking about those for whom they were ultimately responsible. He wished to remove the apparently authoritative cosmetic surface of these institutions to show the heartless void within.

Yet penetrating beneath the surface must not be thought of as Dickens' prerogative alone. The idea of unmasking gives us a useful metaphor by which to suggest how interpretative reading can work. It indicates how we, too, can uncover the beliefs which lie beneath the surface of a text: beliefs about how individuals and societies function; beliefs which inform how, at a certain moment in literary history, a story is told, a character is constructed. Such critical exposure of assumptions can reveal a decided tension between what the surface of a novel—the remarks made in the omniscient narrative voice, say—*appears* to tell us, and what an examination of the language in which events and attitudes are written about in fact shows to be the case.

Moreover, it can be equally illuminating to look at what is *not* said by an author. Such reading of the gaps, of the text's *un*said, can point up two things in particular: what a writer takes unquestioningly for granted as 'natural', as unquestionable, at the time and for the society within which he or she is writing; and additionally what, consciously or unconsciously, he or she suppresses: suppresses since the concepts raised are awkward or unmanageable, or—particularly one might say, where sexuality inserts itself into the Victorian bourgeois novel—unthinkable.[2]

This type of unmasking analysis may be approached in two different ways. The first of these operates on what may be called a horizontal, or *synchronic* axis, tracing analogies, and hence highlighting contradictions across the whole body of Dickens' text. It thus makes it hard—if not impossible—to determine with the confidence shown by some critics that the novels of this particular author embody consistent points of view. Such reading, on a synchronic axis, invariably must be a process which takes no substantial account of history, whether of the chronology of Dickens' work and experience, or of the difference in expectations between the Victorian consumer and ourselves. Indeed, it is a mode of analysis which stresses our response today, and is incomplete, I would suggest, without historical contextualisation. One approach to such contextualisation can be found in the second mode of unmasking. This *diachronic* method—a method which takes full account of historical change—involves considering that since we are looking back on the texts after an interval of some 140 years, certain attitudes have become more questionable or more obvious. To read with attention to historical perspective, in other words, means more than trying to understand the novels in relation to the time at which they originally appeared, but has to do with the development of our own social and literary assumptions. This looking back at the difference between what Robert Weimann has called 'past significance and present meaning'[3] is a good way by which, at a simple level, the text's *un*spoken may be made to speak.

This diachronic method can be seen in operation if we focus on the one agent of social control for which Dickens seemed to possess genuine admiration: the Metropolitan Police. We meet it both in the person of Inspector Field, who accompanied Dickens' nocturnal visits round the notorious criminal neighbourhood of London's Seven Dials, and in his fictional counterparts, the diligent Bucket of *Bleak House* and the Night Inspector of *Our Mutual Friend*.[4] Yet looking back from the late twentieth century we may find much to question in the police powers, the authority which Dickens appears to take absolutely for granted. Rightly, he pointed to the detective police's intimate knowledge of an area and its inhabitants, but also accepts without a qualm the blithe assumption on their part—not to mention that of their literary guest—that they could enter a lodging house at will, at any time of day or night, and sniff around, in partly paternalistic, certainly suspicious surveillance. Similarly Bucket, in *Bleak House*, seems able to penetrate, effortlessly, into any home, that inviolable sanctuary elsewhere in

Dickens' writings. The ranging, piercing capacity of his 'sharp eye', concealed somewhat by verbal blandishments, may not be comfortable, but it is never suggested that it is not necessary, whether in the cause of justice or plot:

> Time and place cannot bind Mr Bucket. Like man in the abstract, he is here today and gone tomorrow—but, very unlike man indeed, he is here again the next day. This evening he will be casually looking into the iron extinguishers at the door of Sir Leicester Dedlock's house in town; and tomorrow morning he will be walking on the leads of Chesney Wold, where erst the old man walked whose host is propitiated with a hundred guineas. Drawers, desks, pockets, all things belonging to him, Mr Bucket examines. (BH: 53)

The authority of the detective and the social structure which it supports hence occupy a position which the text never openly questions. It is up to us to reveal such positions, to query, indeed, the authority of the text to speak definitively in the way in which it seems to do, and it is easiest to practise this when we can stand at some distance—temporal, ideological, or both—from the attitudes which the texts embody. This will involve not just a knowledge of rapidly altering material conditions, and of changing social assumptions, but the bringing of an awareness of the changing use of language, and of different literary conventions and expectations, to bear on the novels.

In the following chapters, these synchronic and diachronic processes will be seen in operation. But let us first turn back to 'The Stroller's Tale', and see how these processes may be applied to what may seem, at a first reading, to be a tangential passage in the novel. The emaciated clown has been presented in starkly shocking terms to us, through the mouthpiece of the dismal man. But he can still somersault away and entertain another audience—albeit one which, it is implied, does not pause to consider what lies beneath the surface of the show. For them, the artiste will have bounded off the stage at the end of his performance, and be seen and thought of no more. We, on the other hand, learn of his return to his death-bed, of his hallucinations, trapped in a labyrinth of contracting and expanding rooms and vaults, surrounded by crawling, glistening, staring insects and reptiles. To the last, the narrator pushes home the theme of ironic contrast: 'I saw the wasted limbs, which a few hours before had been distorted for the amusement of a boisterous gallery, writhing under the tortures of a burning fever; I heard the clown's shrill laugh blending with the low murmurings of the dying man' (PP: 3).

Pickwick is spared from having to respond to the chilling vignette by the entrance of his friends. This is a fictional device by which Dickens, too, evades the problem both of utterance, in the form of authorial comment, and of considering not only what would be a credible psychological response on Pickwick's part, but how to integrate such a response with the tone of the relatively jolly, picaresque jaunt which he had established in the first two chapters. But with careful reading, we can pass quickly beyond the absence of overt authorial comment. 'The Stroller's Tale' becomes, through its positioning, what we may call self-referential. Ostensibly about a single clown, it can also be seen to act as a metaphor for how we read the whole novel: a metaphor probably not consciously designed by Dickens (though we can never prove this one way or the other), but none the less effective. Just as the clown's audience do not want to think on two levels at once, to consider what lies behind his performance, so it is far easier to follow a simple narrative continuum, to enjoy the energetic adventures of Pickwick, Snodgrass, Winkle and co., than it is to pause on an episode which is, in narrative and tonal terms, jarring. But we must consider the cumulative effect of reading the whole novel, with the impact made by subsequent interpolated tales—the violent wife-beating of 'The Convict's Return' (PP: 6); the visions which assault the sulky, drunken Gabriel Grub in 'The Story of the Goblins who Stole a Sexton' (PP: 29), and the way these combine with the darker elements which develop in the mainstream of the story. Then we can think back to the implications of our response to the clown, to the importance of attending to the social realities on which entertainment, both fictional and theatrical, ultimately depend.

The seriousness of these realities is made explicit by Dickens in the main story at the moment when Pickwick is imprisoned for debt in the Fleet. The novelist here assumes his public tone, an amalgam of the orator and leader writer. Although (writing in 1837) debtors were no longer suspended in an iron cage on the Fleet wall to appeal for alms, the condition of such prisoners was still a questionable one:

> we still leave unblotted in the leaves of our statute book, for the reverence and admiration of succeeding ages, the just and wholesome law which declares that the sturdy felon shall be fed and clothed, and that the penniless debtor shall be left to die of starvation and nakedness. This is no fiction. (PP: 42)

In recalling the hungry-looking man rattling the money-box on the Fleet wall, Dickens appeals to his own audience's awareness of historical change: 'Most of our readers will remember' this pauper's presence 'until within a very few years past'. But in adding his commentary on the state of things, he reminds them that they have no cause for complacency, that there must be change still to come. This process is inevitable as well as, in this case, desirable. And this serves to emphasise that second important way in which Dickens' texts should be read: in the full consciousness of historical perspective.

Earlier, I suggested that both Dickens and we, the readers, are concerned with processes of unmasking. What is certain is that at no time, then or now, have there been fixed, absolute meanings to be discovered. Reading, whether we speak literally of our own practice with texts, or figuratively, as in Dickens' application of imagination and interpretation to society and its constituent individuals, will offer no unified, consistent answers. The idea of contradiction, which I have advanced in this chapter as a central characteristic of Dickens' writing is, for example, in no way an explanation of his work. It serves merely as one concept among many— albeit a highly useful one—which one can apply as a tool, to see what it reveals about the texts. For, as we shall see in subsequent chapters, Dickens is an author whose writings continually contradict themselves. Moreover, this contradiction is a pattern which goes far beyond attitudes to specific issues, such as home or imprisonment, industry or the pastoral. It extends to tone, to the alternation of optimism and pessimism, comedy and tragedy, to the variety of voices which are heard within Dickens' novels.

This, of course, makes it extremely hard to generalise about Dickens' fiction, and illustrates easily the fact that these texts readily support a plurality of interpretations, which need not be mutually exclusive, nor rankable in any order of preference. Take *The Old Curiosity Shop* as an example of a novel which not only has been subjected to a wide variety of approaches—all literary works, after all, have this potential— but which has given rise to a widely differing assortment of apparently absolute interpretations. Even before Oscar Wilde's caustic comment that one would 'need a heart of stone not to laugh at the death of Little Nell',[5] the book had become something of a byword for what Aldous Huxley was to term 'pathological sentimentality'.[6] Fitzjames Stephen, for example, calling the young girl's demise one 'over which so many foolish tears have been shed', commented with considerable distaste that Dickens 'gloats over the girl's death as if it delighted him; he looks at it . . . touches, tastes, smells and handles as if it were some savoury dainty which could not be too fully appreciated.'[17]

Yet more recently, criticism has worked to reappropriate Nell's death. It has been set in an historical context, pandering to a Victorian penchant for weepy literary death-beds in a period when child mortality, and a subsequent need for consolation, was more common than today. In literary historical terms, it has been seen as belonging both to the strand of English romantic tradition which stressed the potential for happiness in death, particularly child death, and to the primitive spirituality found in German popular romances.[8] In a biographical context, critics have drawn attention to Dickens' distress at the early death of his sister-in-law, Mary Hogarth—an interpretation which shades into the psychoanalytic, pointing to the cathartic effect, for both writer and reader, of released emotion.

Other studies, whether from embarrassment or boredom, have tried to bypass the overstated morbidity of the individual case of Nell, and have looked for wider resonances. Edgar Johnson, for example, examines the commercial and economic implications;[9] and Schwarzbach has amplified these by suggesting that Nell's desire to beg, or work in a non-cash economy, bartering work for food and shelter, is the only means which will allow her to remain uncontaminated. The novel, for him, has something to say about Dickens' attitude towards capitalist society. This can be exemplified, for instance, by looking at the passage where Nell and her grandfather, fleeing London, pass into 'the haunts of commerce and great traffic':

> The old man looked about him with a startled and bewildered gaze, for these were places that he hoped to shun. He pressed his finger on his lip, and drew the child along by narrow courts and

winding ways, nor did he seem at ease until they had left it far behind, often casting a backward look towards it, murmuring that ruin and self-murder were crouching in every street, and would follow if they scented them; and that they could not fly too fast. (OCS: 15)

Such a passage, describing in terms of biblical solemnity the flight from the City of Destruction, can persuasively be used to point to a thematic connection between death and commerce, allowing the novel to be viewed as an escapist and retrogressive attempt to avoid the effects and implications of developing capitalism.[10]

Reading *The Old Curiosity Shop*, one can hardly ignore the omnipresence of the gloomy side of death, the magnetic force which, on Nell's travels, seems to pull her towards a place's oldest inhabitants, tending, even digging graves. Even when the reader is equipped either with first-hand, or subsequently acquired statistical knowledge of the London mortality figures, it seems just Nell's luck that, gazing out onto the busy streets around the shop, she would 'perhaps see a man passing with a coffin on his back, and two or three others silently following him to a house where somebody lay dead' (OCS: 9). But not all the references are on this sobering level. With greater equilibrium than occurs within the pointed irony of 'The Stroller's Tale', Dickens mingles the comic and grotesque with churchyard peace by placing Punch crosslegged on a tombstone, 'pointing with the tip of his cap to a most flourishing epitaph'. With even greater irreverence, he introduces the clergyman's horse, which 'stumbling with a dull blunt sound among the graves, was cropping the grass; at once deriving orthodox consolation from the dead parishioners, and enforcing last Sunday's text that this was what all flesh came to' (OCS: 16). As well as alleviating the odour of piety which accumulates round Nell whenever she enters the presence of death, such moments remind the reader that there is more than one way of looking at a gravestone. Indeed, the novel is to some extent structured around the principle of opposites. The incidents in the ostensibly secondary plot, which juxtapose and offset the story of the girl and her grandfather, remind us that within the polarised terms of the underpinning mythology, we must accept that if the adolescent Nell is fit, in her moral and physical purity, to take her place among the angels, that there are unrestful berths waiting in the other place for such as the cruelly sadistic Quilp.

Irresolvable contradictions are found throughout Dickens' fictions. Even allowing for what appears to be a growing pessimism in his personal attitudes, there is, as critics have long noticed, a divide between the belief, as expressed in his fiction, that the individual human heart can and does change; and the intense despair which comes over him when he examines society as a whole. In *Our Mutual Friend*, for example, his last completed novel, we see the first of these precepts in operation. Bella is educated out of being a doubly spoilt girl: spoilt first by poverty and then by wealth; and Eugene Wrayburn is rescued by Lizzie Hexham from death by drowning and redeemed from his 'negligent reckless' self, a prey to 'consummate indolence', to be a socially responsible human. But this process of transformation rubs up against the opinions which Dickens voiced privately—as to W.C. Macready, complaining that he believed, reluctantly, that 'the English people are habitually consenting parties to the miserable imbecility into which we have fallen, *and never will help themselves out of it*'.[11] His overt fictional adherence to the principle of private goodness of heart persists, despite Dickens' first-hand knowledge of appalling slum conditions, and of monolithic, inefficient systems of administration, neither of which would be transformed overnight, or even in a few years, through the reformation of individual sentiment. As Susan R. Horton points out in *The Reader in the Dickens*

World, there was a considerable gap between what Dickens wanted to be true, and what his perceptions told him really was the case.[12]

Duality is apparent in Dickens' non-fictional writing as well as in his novels. In letters and speeches, and in the prefaces to individual novels, Dickens frequently expresses what, he claims, are the aims which motivate him. Like the eighteenth-century novelists he so much admired—Defoe, Fielding and Smollett—he wished both to entertain ('to contribute, as far as in me lies, to the common stock of healthful cheerfulness and enjoyment'[13]) and to instruct ('we cannot hold in too strong a light of disgust and contempt, before the view of others, all meanness, falsehood, cruelty, and oppression, of every grade and kind'[14]). Of course, statements of intentionality are notoriously unreliable, written, as they tend to be, with fore-or hind-sight. Moreover, as we shall see, there is no logical reason why statements about fiction should be assumed to carry any more validity than the fiction itself, especially considering that, as is the case with all utterances, there is always the audience to be considered, and Dickens, in the case of the two clear declarations just quoted, could well be described as packaging himself, and simplifying his attitudes, in order to please his American readership. That he was capable of this is demonstrated when a speech which he made on the 1842 tour, acclaiming 'your enlightened care for the happiness of the many, your tender and gentle regard for the afflicted and helpless',[15] is placed against his attacks on American civic irresponsibility, first in *American Notes* and then, more forceably, in *Martin Chuzzlewit*. Other instances can be added which show that Dickens is not to be relied on as a witness when it comes to his own writing.

Take, for example, his visit to Preston in early 1854. Dickens denied vehemently to the critic, Peter Cunningham, that his visit had anything to do with the novel. He claimed that it was a mischief to lead the public to suppose that it did, since this encouraged them to 'believe in the impossibility that books are produced in that very sudden and cavalier manner (as poor Newton used to feign that he produced the elaborate drawings he made in his madness, by winking at the table)'.[16] Additionally—the social implications being as important to Dickens as the aesthetic ones—Cunningham's drawing attention to his visit could damage the story's didactic potential, since it 'localises ... a story which has a direct purpose in reference to the working people all over England'.[17] Yet, as pp. 108–10 demonstrate, there are strong parallels to be drawn between Dickens' article 'On Strike' for *Household Words*, which explicitly describes the state of affairs in Preston, and the trade union meeting in *Hard Times*. No amount of difference in emphasis can hide these similarities.

But it seems hard to deny that the emphatic feelings about the purpose of his writing, which Dickens expressed on many occasions, correlate with the opinions, subject-matter and narrative address of his fiction. One of his firm beliefs, which he shared with many Victorian critics, was that there were some matters which were suitable for fiction, others which were not. He shared, for example, the prevalent middle-class criterion that novels should be safely consumable by all family members. But if he and his contemporaries found a notable difference between fiction and non-fiction, it does not necessarily follow that we should apply different modes of analysis to each, particularly when Dickens habitually uses language—however rich in startling metaphor it may be— with reference to a factual discourse, an assumed world of observable, experiential things. All his writing contains potential ambiguities, inconsistencies and complex effects, and a rhetorical analysis which draws out an awareness of these possibilities can be applied to all his work, as to similar texts: *Little Dorrit* or Elizabeth Gaskell's *Mary Barton*; articles in *Household Words* or the 1848 *Report of the Metropolitan Sanitary Commissioners*.

By using the proposition that there is no fundamental difference, in this case, between the rhetorical approach to so-called fictitious and non-fictitious texts, and joining it to an idea put forward much earlier in this chapter, that one aspect of Dickens' writing can be used to point up telling inconsistencies or ambiguities elsewhere, we can examine a passage from 'Meditations in Monmouth Street', one of the *Sketches by Boz*, the articles which appeared in the *Morning Chronicle* and *Evening Chronicle* between 1834 and 1836. Dickens speculates about the previous wearers of the clothes which hang in the dealers' shops, tracing imaginary life-histories from the hints offered by worn corduroys, black office suits, and a broad-skirted coat with large metal buttons. Though the garments are on simultaneous display, he invents the progress of a human through decent boyhood, his employment as a message boy, his increasing lack of care for his anxious, widowed mother, and the way in which he passes into a rapid moral decline:

> These things happen every hour, and we all know it; and yet we felt as much sorrow when we saw, or fancied we saw—it makes no difference which—the change that began to take place now, as if we had just conceived the bare possibility of such a thing for the first time. The next suit, smart but slovenly; meant to be gay and yet not half so decent as the threadbare apparel; redolent of the idle lounge, and the blackguard companions, told us, we thought, that the widow's comfort had rapidly faded away. (SB: p. 76)

And so on down: the man passes through rakishness, to wife-beater, father of a sickly, hungry family, his dying mother lying in a metropolitan workhouse.

The crucial phrase in this is 'we saw, or fancied we saw—it makes no difference which—'. This suggests that it is difficult to draw an easy distinction between fact and fiction when it

45

comes to Dickens' work. It renders his observation of actual objects on sale in an identifiable London location on a par with his imaginings and, simultaneously, gives the status of verifiable truth to what one might presume to be imagined accumulations of detail in the packed descriptive passages in his novels.[18]

The dividing line between invention and personal observation becomes an impossible one to draw: one more fact which highlights the uncertainty inherent in the whole practice of criticism. Perhaps one conclusion which we may safely reach, however, is that in pointing to the contradictions in Dickens' writings we must not fall into the trap of thinking that their presence is always unconscious. They are, frequently, a deliberate manifestation of Dickens' use of rhetorical effects. He was acutely aware of the importance of such effects, of the need to play on his readers, to rouse their responses, to keep them entertained and alert, so that they would listen and, for that matter, keep purchasing. In the following chapter, I wish to examine some of these varieties of effects and addresses which the novels contain.

3

Dickens' Narratives: Voice and Variation

Dickens' plots are always complicated. Indeed, none of his novels contains just one plot, one centre of interest, although our attention may be focused more consistently on Oliver Twist, say, than on Nancy and Bill Sikes; on Little Nell than on Dick Swiveller and the Marchioness. Not only does the text shift from one group of characters, one embodiment of a theme to another, but its tone often alters too: from descriptive to satiric, from exhortatory to sentimental. In this chapter, I wish not just to look at some of these alternations which take place within the text, and at their effect on the reader, but also to offer some terms from narrative theory which can be useful when describing these frequent movements of attention and tone.

As a novelist, Dickens has much in common with Dostoevsky. Both are fascinated by extremes of emotion, by the urban experience, by violence and crime. Both crowd their novels with characters, details and descriptions, and organise their fictions in similar ways. The Russian formalist critic, Mikhail Bakhtin, recognised a 'plurality of independent

47

and unmerged voices and consciousnesses'[1] in Dostoevsky's writings: a plurality which can easily be seen in Dickens' works, too. Bakhtin proposed the concept of the 'dialogic' or 'polyphonic' novel to describe this type of fictional treatment: that is, a novel which functions according to more than one scheme of logic; which has more than one voice to be listened to within it.

The overriding characteristic of the dialogic imagination is that it admits and presents unresolvable differences and points of view. The novels of Dickens which at a cursory glance might appear to come closest to denying this, to maintaining a monologic viewpoint, are those which are told in the first person: *David Copperfield* and *Great Expectations*. Yet our experience of reading these shows immediately that this idea of their being unified by the voice of a named teller is a chimera.

How, then, in the case of these first-person narratives can we describe their lack of cohesion? First, there is the split which occurs between what may be termed the *narrator*, whose telling of the story coincides, in fictional time, with putting it to paper; and the *focaliser*, whose point of view coincides with the experiencing of an event, the observation of a scene in the fictional past. Thus, when the adult David recalls his 'earliest remembrance' of his childhood home, and mentions the 'great dog-kennel in a corner, without any dog: and a quantity of fowls that look terribly tall to me, walking about, in a menacing and ferocious manner' (DC: 2), he is clearly not using the vocabulary of the *focaliser*, even though he is adopting his perspective. No more is the narrator of *Great Expectations*, recollecting the young Pip's fear of Magwitch ('I was in mortal terror of my interlocutor with the ironed leg' (GE: 2)); he uses a deliberately sophisticated vocabulary which demonstrates his distance from the child he once was. *David Copperfield* is, in this narrative respect, the more complex of the two texts, since the adult David claims omniscience over the state of his mother's mind whilst alone, pregnant with him, looking at the fire 'through her tears, and desponding heavily about herself and the fatherless little stranger' (DC: 1). This may represent the grown man using his imagination, but the effect is as though a third narrative position has crept in, sharing the vocabulary of the *narrator*, but no perspective ever available to the *focaliser*.

In these two texts, it is necessarily the *narrator* who adds touches of nostalgia, describing Pip, for example, as he journeys towards London: 'We changed again, and yet again, and it was now too late and too far to go back, and I went on. And the mists had all solemnly risen now, and the world lay spread before me' (GE: 19). The later voice, too, is in possession of the literary competence which ties this in with Milton's Adam and Eve making their wandering steps and slow away from the irrecoverable innocence of Eden. It is the *narrator* who utters prophetic comments in a tone of rueful hindsight. The adult David describes little Em'ly springing along a decrepit wooden jetty:

> there have been times since, in my manhood, many times there have been, when I have thought, Is it possible, among the possibilities of hidden things, that in the sudden rashness of the child and her wild look so far off, there was any merciful attraction of her into danger, any tempting her towards him permitted on the part of her dead father, that her life might have a chance of ending that day? (DC: 3)

Although, when the sentence is completed, and when one gives weight to the word 'merciful', it is clear that the pronoun 'him' refers to her 'drowndead' parent, for an instant, before the convoluted phrasing is played out, it seems to refer to a hitherto unintroduced male seducer, a fleeting syntactical prefiguration of Steerforth. Such passages enable the reader to read on in possession of more knowledge, more curiosity, and perhaps more apprehension, than the *focaliser*.

This gap between *narrator* and *focaliser* reminds us how tenuous a coherence is the 'I' of any writing, whether fiction or autobiography. As a pronoun, it gives an apparent cohesion to a text; it is the means which a writer or speaker, real or imaginary, employs to bring a sense of cohesion to his or her own life. Moreover, the gap allows the reader to stand back, in the case of both David and Pip, and take note of their growth to self-knowledge. In the case of David's relationship to Agnes, this is made exasperatingly clear. As early as Chapter 18, the *focaliser* is perceiving her, now grown 'quite a woman', as 'the better angel of the lives of all who come within her calm, good, self-denying influence'. The implications are clear to the reader once David reveals his compulsion to write to her 'as soon as Dora and I were engaged ... I remember that I sat resting my head upon my hand, when the letter was half done, cherishing a general fancy as if Agnes were one of the elements of my natural home' (DC: 34). No further effort is demanded of the reader than to wait and observe how the apparently inevitable conclusion is arrived at, and to take pleasure at the *focaliser* recognising that he has that knowledge which has long been in the possession of the reader.

One can argue that there is another form of double logic operating within these two novels which also undermines the apparent unity given by employing a first-person narrative. This is the same double logic that operates within any nineteenth-century fiction in which the plot is presented in terms of sequences of events which are dependent on a process of cause and effect. Pip is largely impelled to become a gentleman by Estella's scornful treatment of him and by the class inferiority which he is made to feel. David meets Dora as a result of working for her father and being invited to the Spenlow house as a matter of courtesy. These events appear to exist prior to, and independently of, their presentation through Pip and David's eyes. Simultaneously, however, it seems that these events are justified—indeed, brought into being—because they serve a thematic structuring of the novel: aiding the presentation of what the text shows to be the true sources of generous and courteous feeling, or of the theme of recognising valuable qualities in one's marriage partner rather than impetuously falling prey to romantic delusions. This is not to suggest, of course, that the novels can be reduced to these themes: indeed, they may not be what now interest us most. But undeniably they are present, and equally undeniably, it is impossible to say whether they produce, or are produced by, the ordering of the plot.

If this chicken-and-egg question arises in relation to the presentation of events, so too does it crop up with regard to the positioning of the author himself. As Jacques Derrida has put it, the authorial centre of a text lies both '*within* the structure and *outside* it'.[2] This is easily seen in the case of the imaginary scribe: David both narrates and is the person things happen to. It is equally true of Dickens: he can be found making utterances, in varied voices, from the position of a narrator within the text—utterances which, when the audience is addressed directly, we have no reason to attribute to an imaginary character and which, indeed, when they are compared with Dickens' tone and opinions in non-fictional pieces, encourage us to identify them with various modes of Dickens' 'own' voice. Indeed, they partly make up our grounds for identifying that entity which we term 'Dickens'. Yet simultaneously, Dickens is the wielder of the pen, the man who planned and phrased the narrator's intervention which came precisely at that point: the overviewer to whom he refers (and which he constructs) in, for example, the postscript to *Our Mutual Friend*, when he hopes that the novel's readers will, now that 'they have it before them complete, perceive the relation of its finer threads to the whole pattern which is always before the eyes of the story-weaver at his loom'. (OMF: Postscript).

But this description of his authorial function, of course, masks Dickens' unarticulated amalgam of assumptions and prejudices, his choice of what may and may not be considered important, which may furthermore be said to be unconsciously present within the text. Even before we reach the subject of Dickens' rapid fluctuations of tone, we can see that the whole concept of a narrator, whether in the first or third person, is a more complex one than appears at first sight.

Certain of Dickens' novels contain elements which positively heighten their dialogic nature. These include the interpolated tales in *Pickwick* and *Nicholas Nickleby*; the way in which Master Humphrey fades from the scene, having introduced and taken a quiet part in the first three chapters of *The Old Curiosity Shop*, and the insertion, verbatim, of Miss Wade's life story in *Little Dorrit*. But the most obviously dialogic of all the novels is *Bleak House*, with Esther's narrative being told in the first person and in the past tense, and the remainder being narrated in a multiplicity of registers and from a kaleidoscope of points of view, in the present tense, and in the third person. We are faced on the one hand with the narrow, personal view, which organises the elements of the story around the part which its narrator plays in it, recounting only events at which she was present, reaching a tidy culmination in her marriage, and in what we hear of her future family. The very fact that this part of the novel speaks in the past tense, that Esther tells us that the events which she has been narrating took place some seven years previously, suggests that experience can be assimilated and ordered. It bears out Steven Marcus's assertion that any form of historical narrative 'offers assurance to its society of readers because the world it represents has already been defined and in some sense closed off; things in it, in other words, have already happened.'[3] This seems initially questionable in the case of some of Dickens' novels. In *A Tale of Two Cities*, for example, the recounting of the revolutionary past clearly prompts readers to be disquietened by contemporary political developments. But it nevertheless remains true that the use of the past tense is one of the means by which an author can appear to bring order to his or her fiction. Indeed, in the case of *A Tale of Two Cities*, one could argue that it is only because past events can apparently be wrapped up in clearcut narrative that they can possibly constitute an effective warning to the present.

The assurance and order offered by Esther's narrative is, however, immediately denied by the more widely ranging chapters which show that the society of *Bleak House* is not one which can speak with a unified, communal, assured voice. Although elements of a particular plot are tidied up at the end of the novel, the general sense of confusion, and of the elements which caused it, remain, as the use of the present tense indicates. There is, at the time of Krook's spontaneous combustion, a tenuous hint offered that in some unspecified, apocalyptic future, moral justice will prevail:

> The Lord Chancellor of that Court, true to his title in his last act, has died the death of all Lord Chancellors in all Courts, and of all authorities in all places under all names soever, where false pretences are made, and where injustice is done. (BH: 32)

This, however, is a nebulous and unverifiable promise. By speaking in the present tense—sometimes the simple present, sometimes the present progressive, sometimes leaving out the verb altogether—the narrative voice of these chapters claims no absolute organising authority. Moreover, it suggests that to claim that life *can* be neatly ordered—as Esther's narrative implicitly does—is a falsification, or at best an acute limitation, of the facts.

Apart from its structural function, Esther's narrative differs from the first-person voice of David or Pip in one important sense. It is that of a woman. Certainly, it is an individualised voice, that of someone who, suffering from early feelings of rejection, and from the fact that she could not understand the mystery and stigma surrounding her birth, is compelled simultaneously to stress her usefulness and sense of duty, and also to indulge in a fair amount of self-abnegation. But the voice also carries an element of typicality. The American writer, Grace Greenwood, reported that Dickens had said to her that the style of Esther's chapters had 'cost him no little labour and anxiety', and he asked 'Is it quite natural, quite girlish?'[4] It would thus seem that not all her coy whimsicalities can be attributed to a traumatic childhood, especially when one considers that she apparently represents one of Dickens' favourite idealised types, jangling that magic talisman of a good housekeeper: a bunch of keys, at her belt.

Esther exemplifies some of what Dickens habitually presented as positive aspects of womanhood. But one can also question whether, in fact, his adoption of a woman's voice is linked in, at a conscious or unconscious level, with the limitations of perspective in her narrative. This sense of limitation is the more noticeable since it operates on a personal as well as on a social plane. It can be seen when we contrast David and Pip, shown to be alert to the spots of blindness earlier in their lives, with the way in which Esther makes her artless references to Woodcourt:

> I have forgotten to mention—at least I have not yet mentioned— that Mr Woodcourt was the same dark young surgeon whom we had met at Mr Badger's. Or, that Mr Jarndyce invited him to dinner that day. Or, that he came. (BH: 14)

She is not relating with hindsight what she did not know, or failed to see, at the time. The concealment is concurrent with the narration, rather than with the perception. It is an indication that she has not yet outgrown her habits of self-concealment, and achieved a total understanding of her earlier behaviour. Such concealment, springing as it does from the quirks of her particular psyche, need not, of course, in itself be gender-specific. But Dickens' insistence on the femininity of Esther's voice suggests that limitation of point of view, here as elsewhere, is a further aspect of her woman-ness.

But it is impossible to divide the complicated structure of *Bleak House* into a neat juxtaposition of Esther's limited (individual, woman's) point of view and the all-seeing, if not all-comprehending (multiple, male) perspective. For the latter invades and occupies the former, thus still further undermining Esther's authority. At times, this occupation is ambiguous. When Esther first stays in the chaotic Jellyby household, tells bed-time stories to the children, tidies Ada's and her own room, enlivens the fire, and eventually returns downstairs:

> I felt that Mrs Jellyby looked down upon me rather, for being so frivolous; and I was sorry for it; though at the same time I knew that I had no higher pretensions. (BH: 4)

Various choices—not necessarily mutually exclusive ones—lie before us as to how to read this. Either it is Esther being honest, and thus exhibiting yet further her meek naivety; or she is conscious of her own ironic tone, and is taking a sly dig at Mrs Jellyby; or there is a wiser narrator standing behind Esther (as he never does in the case of David and Pip), not just showing up her limitations by juxtaposing her with a far more mobile, multivocal consciousness in the structure of the book, but, as here, by introducing apparently unconscious irony.

The presence of the invading narrator is felt yet more strongly in the next chapter, when Esther and her companions visit Krook's shop. We read a lively listing of the

rags and parchment scrolls; an enumeration and contextualisation of the

> quantities of dirty bottles: blacking bottles, medicine bottles,
> ginger-beer and soda-water bottles, pickle bottles, wine bottles,
> ink bottles: I am reminded by mentioning the latter, that the shop
> had, in several particulars, the air of being in a legal neighbour-
> hood, and of being, as it were, a dirty hanger-on and disowned
> relation of the law. (BH: 5).

The only hint of the voice which we have come to call
Esther's in this occurs in the apparent vagueness of London
topography—'the air of being in a legal neighbourhood'—but
even this innocence is undercut by the fact that, in the first
sentence of the next paragraph, she has no trouble in
recognising that 'the shop was blinded... by the wall of
Lincoln's Inn'. The voice, rather, can be equated with that of
the omniscient text, with its frequent passages of crowded
description—not to mention, if we choose, with the voice of
the Dickens of *Sketches by Boz*. Esther, in other words, has no
consistent voice herself and, one could argue, therefore is, in
fact, no more stable a character than the constantly shifting
omniscient narrator himself. She appears only *as* a
character—indeed, is only gendered—when the voice
accredited to her places its emphasis in a certain way. Instead
of representing a clearcut dichotomy between personal and
impersonal methods of telling a story and describing a
society, the presence of Esther's voice is just one more of
those transient voices which are heard throughout the text—
voices of public exhortation, of melodrama and suspense, of
religious satire, of social anger, and of perpetual amusement
at varieties of human frailty.

Division of attention is an inevitable part of reading any
multi-plot novel. It is something deliberately encouraged by
the structure of the opening chapters of many of Dickens'

works. Take *The Old Curiosity Shop*. If one first pays attention to the preface to the first cheap edition (1848), (reading the novel in volume form, rather than in weekly parts, in which the sense of dislocation would be necessarily yet more pronounced) this has the advantage of preparing us for the odd manner in which Master Humphrey begins the narration in his own voice, and then precipitously, and permanently, vanishes from the text. But we also find Dickens claiming that:

> I had it always in my fancy to surround the lonely figure of the child with grotesque and wild but no impossible companions, and to gather about her innocent face and pure intentions, associates as strange and uncongenial as the grim objects that are about her bed when her history is first foreshadowed.

Yet this gives what proved to be a misleading impression of unity: a Nell-centric vision. In the opening numbers, her pious timidity is little imaginative match for the strength of Quilp's gloating maliciousness; for the diabolic greed with which he both crunches through hard-boiled eggs, shells and all, and with which he hungrily smacks his lips at the female sex. And, as with picaresque novels, the energetic novelty of those encountered on the road—troupes of performing dogs, giants on stilts, Mrs Jarley's waxworks—has the effect not just again of thrusting Nell into the background, but of temporarily halting the narration. They demand attention as separate vignettes, treated in much the same way as Boz's journalistic set-pieces, or as the varied gallery of types recorded by Henry Mayhew in his *London Labour and the London Poor*.

Three more examples reinforce the way in which the differing foci of opening chapters make it hard to settle down into one train of reading. The beginning of *Little Dorrit* jumps from the Marseilles prison to the Marseilles quarantine. Even without knowledge of the repeated motif of incarceration in the novel, we can see that here are two different types of confinement, but otherwise can make no other link. Rather, we store the juxtaposition, trusting the relevance of the first chapter, and that the personages introduced in it will have some bearing on the story/stories that later unfold—although, as the disappearing Master Humphrey warns us, this might be a dangerous assumption to hold. Arguably it is hindsight, as well as habits of reading, which make it justifiable. The opening chapters of *Our Mutual Friend* are particularly unsettling for a reader looking for one line to follow. They pass from the macabre fishing activities on the dark Thames in the first chapter, outlined through melodramatic suggestion; to the Veneerings' dinner party, introduced in terms instantly recognisable as satiric: 'Mr and Mrs Veneering were bran-new people in a bran-new house in a bran-new quarter of London...' (OMF: I,2). The third chapter seems to make use of this juxtaposition by finding a reason for two characters to leave the dinner-table and travel down to Rotherhithe; but Chapter 4, introducing the Wilfer family in humorous, but not cutting terms, disrupts one's reading yet again through introducing more people; another style. With *Dombey and Son*, even the first few pages demand alertness on the reader's part. The jovial expectations of the first paragraph—Son, newly born, tucked up in a basket bedstead 'immediately in front of the fire and close to it, as if his constitution were analogous to that of a muffin, and it was essential to toast him brown while he was very new'—alters swiftly when one is told, critically, of Dombey's single-minded commercialism: 'Dombey and Son had often dealt in hides, but never in hearts' (DS: 1). By the time of Paul's mother's death at the end of the first chapter, our perspective on the infant has been radically shifted, from comic to serious.

The lack of unity within Dickens' novels seems always to

have worried critics, from the nineteenth century onward. George Brimley, for example, reviewing *Bleak House* in the *Spectator*, held to the principle that: 'We estimate works of art ... more by their unity and completeness than by their richness and profusion of raw materials', and hence attacked the novel: 'even more than any of its predecessors', it is chargeable not with single faults, but with absolute want of construction'.[5] In the case of many of his earlier novels, most frequently in his appended prefaces, Dickens had tried to cover himself against such criticism by claiming that each work had a particular focus. When introducing *Martin Chuzzlewit*, for example, he claimed that he set out 'with the design of exhibiting, in various aspects, the commonest of all the vices', selfishness (MC: Preface).

But such prefatory remarks can in fact be undermined by the experience of reading. Even a sub-title, in the case of *Oliver Twist*, can prove—perhaps deliberately—to be misleading, raising genre expectations which are then subverted. 'A Parish Boy's Progress' suggests a cross between Bunyan, and eighteenth-century moral tales of Industrious and Idle Apprentices. A contemporary reader might have expected to see the hero rising from poverty, struggling determinedly through difficulties. In his 1841 preface to the novel (the most extended defence of any of his fictions) Dickens claimed that he 'wished to show, in little Oliver, the principle of Good surviving through every adverse circumstance, and triumphing at last'. But 'surviving' is hardly an energetic verb. If anyone is educated by the story, it is the reader rather than the protagonist—learning in the earlier parts of the story to feel sympathy and charity for the poor; forced to consider their position on the new Poor Law (the publication of *Oliver* coincided with considerable press controversy, particularly in *The Times* and *Morning Chronicle*, over its operation); forcibly reminded of the lively threat presented by London's criminal population; and led, providing, of course, that their imaginative sympathy has not fallen prey to the energetic, dangerous attraction offered by the prose which describes Fagin and his gang,[6] to see the full power of the quiet, unobtrusive Good of the Maylies and Mr Brownlow, into whose care Oliver was delivered 'by a stronger hand than chance' (OT: 49). Oliver's final triumph is due to others uncovering the mystery of his birth, as well as to his natural goodness arousing Nancy's sympathy, rather than to any unflagging efforts on his part.

How, then, can we best approach Dickens' multi-stranded, mutli-vocal fictions? Those critics who have attempted to impose unificatory lines of interpretation on them (whether influenced by the writer's prefatory comments or not) have invariably found much of the power of the texts eluding them. It is preferable to look for strategies of reading which, though certainly not exhaustive in themselves, can help to highlight both the ways in which Dickens imposes some order on this variety, and also the way in which so much in his writing eludes such means of ordering.

The case of *Oliver Twist*'s sub-title reminds us how problematic it can be to approach a text with preconceptions based on genre expectations, expectations generated by a work being labelled a comedy or a tragedy, a moral fable or a true story. We can be in danger of judging a work according to some pre-existing standard already fixed in our own minds. None the less, it can be useful to see how Dickens drew from types of narrative which were already familiar to him and his readers. We find both that he played on their expectations, manipulating them for his own ends and, simultaneously, that any such attempt to describe one of his novels according to the familiar narrative pattern from which he borrowed leaves a great deal unspoken for.

This can be seen particularly effectively in the case of the mystery story. The process by which we attempt to make sense of a Dickens novel is, on the surface, in many ways like tackling a story of this type: discovering how the apparently disparate characters and scenes are made to fit together, by manipulation of both plot and theme.

Like any writer of such work, Dickens conceals countless details from us. Some of these have their origins in the imaginary time before the story starts. Smike, we learn only late in the novel, is the son of his persecutor, Ralph Nickleby. When 'Mrs Pegler' reveals herself to be Bounderby's mother, she blows the gaffe on his claim to have been born in a ditch and brought up by a drunken grandmother. Other mysteries, like the name of Pip's benefactor, are generated in the course of the story. Sometimes the concealment reminds us of the story's fictionality, since the actions described mimic the narrator's hiding of information from us. We do not learn for some time what is contained in the notes concerning Jonas Chuzzlewit which Nadgett hands over to his employer; he prefers the written form to word of mouth, he says, since you never know who may be listening. The clarification of such details, as here, does not necessarily lie at the centre of the novel. Sorting out the circumstances surrounding Haredale's murder, for example, and the apparently inexplicable attack on the unnamed stranger discovered in the third chapter of *Barnaby Rudge*, do no dominate in the way that the unsolved *Mystery of Edwin Drood* promises to pivot round the disappearance of Edwin. However, all these instances serve a thematic purpose, providing a reminder of how the past can catch up with the present.

However, it is not just with *Edwin Drood*, a novel composed, so far as it goes, very much according to the contemporary fashion for mystery and suspense, that we find an act of concealment dominating the book. A conspicuous instance is the deception played by Boffin on both Bella and the reader in *Our Mutual Friend*. This is so consistent and convincing that critics could speculate whether or not Dickens changed his mind half-way through writing ('one is tempted to wonder whether Dickens did not mean to be genuine and only changed his mind towards the end',[7] hypothesised Humphry House) until Fr. Xavier Shea, through his examination of the novel's number plans, proved this conclusively not to be the case.[8] Indeed, there are two mystery plots operating within *Our Mutual Friend*, but the heavy hints which are dropped about the identity of Rokesmith/Harmon/Hanford function as a decoy for the reader. Our readerly conceit snaps up Rokesmith's 'constrained' and 'troubled' manner when he first meets Bella; smells a rat at the coincidence of his finding both a room at the Wilfers and work with the Boffins; has its suspicions confirmed by the way the writing suggests that there is something strange in the manner in which Rokesmith looks around Boffin's Bower.

Having seen through one puzzle, we thus develop a smug confidence, and are diverted away from the possibility that there may be another one at hand. It is not easy, after all, to suspect Boffin of being 'true golden gold at heart', when the satiric centre of the novel, with the Veneerings and the conspiratorially mercenary Lammles, the greed of Wegg, even the wider operation of, say, the orphan market, all work together to reinforce the moral that wealth corrupts. This moral is strengthened by the excitement and invention which mark the writing in the miserly passages, whether we are learning of the behaviour of Boffin or of Daniel Dancer.[9] And Boffin's performance seems the more plausible, too, because we see it from a variety of perspectives, through the eyes of those he gulls—whether Bella, or Wegg and Venus, or the Lammles. Only once do we observe his miserliness when there are no witnesses, as he leaves Venus's shop, meditating to himself whether or not Venus is planning to get the better of Wegg—a perfectly reasonable speculation, whatever character he might be putting forward. The narrator's subsequent comment is what directs the reader to an interpretation of Boffin's state of mind:

> It was a cunning and suspicious idea, quite in the way of his school of Misers, and he looked very cunning and suspicious as he went jogging through the streets. More than once or twice, more than twice or thrice, say half a dozen times, he took his stick from the arm on which he nursed it, and hit a straight sharp rap at the air with its head. Possibly the wooden countenance of Mr Silas Wegg was incorporeally before him at those moments, for he hit with intense satisfaction. (OMF: III,14)

But Dickens is careful here not to commit himself too absolutely: both the words 'looked' and 'possibly' are used. If anyone is taken in, it must be the reader. For *Our Mutual Friend* is a novel, like *Oliver Twist*, where the reader him-or herself is educated alongside, in this case, several of the central protagonists. And the education takes place this time not through watching a procession of scenes, but through the way one is caught up in the actual process of reading. Bella learns that greed and materialism can corrupt, change, dehumanise a person, and, through a combination of influences (Boffin's performance, Rokesmith, Lizzie) comes to value love and the human affections above money. But the reader's lesson is different: we learn of the danger of making easy judgements, and this applies not just to the individual case of the Golden Dustman, but, by implication, to one's reading of all fiction.

To use the concept of the mystery novel as one possible entrée into Dickens' novels is not, of course, a new one. It has been used, for example, by Viktor Sklovskij, in relation to *Little Dorrit*, a novel in which mystery and concealment are probably less central to the overall thematic concern than in *Our Mutual Friend*, but in which they are still, none the less, important to the construction of the plots. Sklovskij's discussion is particularly useful in that it shows how reading a novel in the light of one genre—in this case, the mystery—can throw up wider issues which help us form a wider terminology, a wider set of distinctions which perhaps may prove useful as one mode of approaching all narratives. He takes *Little Dorrit* as the means by which to illustrate the crucial distinction made by Russian formalists, including himself, when discussing narrative: that between *fabula* and *sjuzet*.[10] *Fabula* describes the raw material of a story: the basic causal–temporal relationships; *sjuzet*, on the other hand, encompasses the story's presentation and manipulation. A marginally more complicated, if similar, set of distinctions is made in structuralist theory, which, in Seymour Chatman's words,

> argues that each narrative has two parts: a story [*histoire*], the content or chain of events (actions, happenings), plus what may be called the existents (characters, items of setting); and a discourse [*discours*], that is, the expression, the means by which the content is communicated. In simple terms, the story is the *what* in a narrative that is depicted, discourse the *how*.[11]

To impose either the formalist or structuralist distinctions wholesale on a text, and to ask no more questions of it, can only lead, of course, to a limited reading. However, it is worth considering what such an attempt to lay bare the mechanics of a text can reveal about it.

The *fabula* of *Little Dorrit*, maintains Sklovskij, is threefold: it comprises the growing relationship and recognition of love between Clennam and Amy; the coming to wealth and subsequent ruin of the Dorrit family; and Rigaud's attempt to blackmail and expose Mrs Clennam. But, says Sklovskij, the novel can be related in such terms only after we have finished reading it. While we read, we have before us a collection of mysteries which help constitute the *sjuzet*: the significance of the watch and case with its embroidered initials; of the mysterious noises in the house; of Affery's 'dreams'. There is the 'heavy labouring on the part of Mr Pancks's machinery' (LD: I,23) to clarify the matter of the Dorrit inheritance, Mr Merdle's secret and, indeed, the precise nature of Clennam and Little Dorrit's feelings for each other—a mystery, to some extent, to Clennam at least, as well as to the reader.

But it would be possible to argue, as Sklovskij fails to do, that the *sjuzet* of *Little Dorrit* encompasses far more than the mystery elements: that considering it involves, for example, Dickens' extended metaphor of imprisonment, which reaches far beyond the Marshalsea—to Mrs Clennam remaining immured and immobile in her room; of Flora, caught in her past, unable to express herself to Clennam except in the disinterred terms of coy romantic intrigues; or Mr Merdle, gloomily holding himself by the wrists as he speaks, as though taking himself into custody.

The mystery plot is undeniably important in a functional sense, forming a means of making and tracing connections between otherwise disparate individuals, just as the enforced quarantine in Marseilles is used as a means to bring Clennam and the Meagles together. But unlike *Bleak House*, with its mystery concerning the past of Lady Dedlock and of Esther's birth, *Little Dorrit* does not in fact use the working-out of its puzzle to underline the wide-reaching lesson of its predecessor: that of the interconnectedness of all parts of society, and the consequent need for the acceptance of mutual responsibility. The mystery plot of the earlier novel provides the means by which, for example, a representative of the aristocracy is brought face to face with brickmakers, with a crossing sweeper. She is both individually dependent upon them, and also is a concrete embodiment of the class which, we have already learnt in more general terms, should be seen to be far more aware of, and to be doing something to remedy, the current grave social problems.

The difference between these two novels can be attributed

in part to a shift in narrative emphasis in Dickens' later fiction. The structure of *Bleak House* demonstrates concern with the perspective of an individual, but uses the limitations of such a viewpoint in conjunction with a wider overview to make a thematic point: the extreme difficulty for any such individual of being able to attain a full perspective on the complexities of contemporary society. Whilst the impetus towards providing some sort of overview is not abandoned by Dickens by any means, the focus of the later novels increasingly stresses the psychological make-up which colours the perspectives which are presented. In *Little Dorrit*, for example, the most important centre of consciousness is, throughout, the subdued, detached, repressed persona of Clennam himself. *David Copperfield* and *Great Expectations* emphasise the moral and social changes of their central protagonists, as, with more varied focal points, does *Our Mutual Friend*, a novel which, in the case of Bradley Headstone, examines the moral deterioration of someone under stress; shows, like the treatment of Jasper in *Edwin Drood*, the intense preoccupations of a mind experiencing extremes of emotion or sensation. Indeed, Dickens' daughter, Kate Perugini, used a crucial phrase when she said of Jasper that 'the originality was to be shown . . . in what we may call *the psychological description* the murderer gives of his temptations, temperament, and character, as if told by another'.[12] In the short first-person narrative, *George Silverman's Explanation* (1867), Dickens experiments with someone so uncertain of himself and, perhaps, aware of the unflattering implications of the tale he has to tell, that he makes several different stabs and from several different angles at opening the damagingly self-revelatory (for Silverman) story: a technique anticipating post-modernist fiction by almost a century. In concentrating on one or several consciousnesses, Dickens' texts come to rest on a belief in the illusory but necessary concept of the integrated human subject. If coherence is not to be found within society as a whole, it may at least be temporarily located within the individual.

The mystery plot of Bleak House may help to connect the worlds of Chesney Wold and Tom-All-Alone's firmly in the reader's mind. Its resolution, as with that of Little Dorrit—or, for that matter, the works of Agatha Christie or P.D. James—grants a certain satisfaction to the reader, giving the impression that it is possible to bring order out of chaos. But this satisfaction is only temporary because, unlike a conventional detective story, there are a large number of loose ends. At the conclusion of Little Dorrit, Clennam and Amy may have a considerable amount of personal strength to go out and face London together, but this, however, does nothing to diminish the alienating potential of the city. Nor, at the end of Bleak House, is any consolation offered in the face of the persistence of the system—whether Chancery, or the government of Coodles and Foodles—and widespread blindness to domestic sanitation problems. However caring and supportive Esther and Woodcourt may be to their family, friends and patients, such activity in the Yorkshire Wolds will do nothing to relieve conditions in the London slums; and in any case, the structure of the novel makes it clear that this rural retreat is the conclusion to only a partial strand of the plot. Recognising Dickens' use of mystery illuminates one reason why, to put it crudely, he wrote such compulsively readable stories. But these fabulae are only part of his dialogic fictions, often not the most memorable part of them. The contradiction remains between Dickens' overall perception of the disparate, unharmonious and continually changing nature of society, and his wish to provide narrative and interpretative systems which can offer some means of making sense of it.

4

Asmodeus Takes the Roofs Off: Narrative Point of View and Contemporary Society

In the previous chapter we looked at various ways in which one can attempt to recognise, and describe, the multiplicity of narrative voices one finds within a Dickens novel. In this chapter, I wish to reintroduce an element of history, to consider that the 'doubt and contradiction and mutability' which, as Barbara Hardy has remarked, the 'largeness and looseness' of Dickens' form allows,[1] may bear a particular relation to the time at which he was writing, and to the predicament in which he found himself as a narrator.

Raymond Williams, in *The Country and the City*, is explicit about linking the form of Dickens' novels to a specific historical and geographical moment:

> Dickens' creation of a new kind of novel ... can be directly
> related to what we must see as [a] double condition: the random
> and the systematic, the visible and the obscured, which is the true
> significance of the city, and especially at this period of the capital
> city, as a dominant social form.. . . It does not matter which
> way we put it: the experience of the city is the fictional method;
> or the fictional method is the experience of the city.[2]

Williams amplifies this by saying that the characteristic moment of a Dickens novel conveys a sense of people rushing by, as in a crowded street. We might remember what Pancks says about Miss Wade's ignorance of her parents: 'They might be in any house she sees, they may be in any churchyard, she passes, she may run against 'em in any street, she may make chance acquaintances of 'em at any time; and never know it' (LD: 2,9). Williams goes on to suggest that the combination of physical noise and bustle in the city, together with the social sense of competition, help determine the way that Dickens' personae characterise themselves in speech, and communicate with one another. This could hardly be called conversation in the conventional sense. Rather, they speak at or past one another, 'in fixed self-descriptions, in voices raised emphatically to be heard through and past similar voices'.[3] The recognition of relationships and connections is forced only slowly out of the consciousness of both characters and readers.

To approach Dickens' writing through this idea of correspondences between fictional form and the society in which and for which it was produced is extremely helpful, particularly in showing how he helps to tame the strangeness of the city by running personal lines of communication across it. We must be careful, however, to see that it is ultimately another form of limited explanation, since it relates the fiction to an assumed 'true' and stable, reportable world outside it. Yet in Chapter 1 we saw how this world was itself made up of multiple ways of perceiving, ordering and recording it; how our access to it is, inevitably, through a series of interpretative readings.

Dickens' own methods of perceiving and ordering his society through his fictions have strong similarities with some of his contemporaries: social investigators whose practice was, it would seem, very different from that of novel writing. I want to arrive at these similarities by examining the use

69

which Dickens makes of the narrative voice within his fiction.

Near the beginning of *A Tale of Two Cities*, an anonymous voice—perhaps that of the narrator, perhaps that of the messenger on horseback—reflects upon the 'wonderful fact'

> that every human creature is constituted to be that profound secret and mystery to every other. A solemn consideration, when I enter a great city by night, that every one of those darkly clustered houses encloses its own secret; that every room in every one of them encloses its own secret; that every beating heart in the hundreds of thousands of breasts there, is, in some of its imaginings, a secret to the heart nearest it! (TTC: 3)

For Dickens, one of the tasks which a narrator can perform is to reveal those closely guarded secrets. The narrator can lift off the roofs of the darkly clustered houses, and adopt a panoramic viewpoint otherwise unavailable within the text: 'Chroniclers are privileged to enter where they list, to come and go through keyholes, to ride upon the wind, to overcome, in their soarings up and down, all obstacles of distance, time and place' (BR: 9). They can make up for deficiencies in the vision and imagination of the individuals they have created. Inspector Bucket, for example, brings the second of these faculties into his search for Lady Dedlock:

> He mounts a high tower in his mind, and looks out far and wide. Many solitary figures he perceives, creeping through the streets; many solitary figures out on heaths, and roads, and lying under haystacks. But the figure that he seeks is not among them. (BH: 56)

Only the narrator can supply her, spotting the lonely woman on the waste by the brick kilns.

Although the social implications of Bucket's speech remain uncommented upon in the text, these nameless, solitary figures have a momentary disruptive effect on Dickens' apparently comprehensive organisation: they are an example of the ease with which issues escape from the frenetic end-tying of his plot. It is clear that the provision of the narrative overview, in its turn, has a social intention which goes beyond a privileged form of spying on personal lives. The prototype of the roof-remover was Asmodeus, the demon in Le Sage's *Diable Boiteux* (1707), who provided his companion, Don Cleofas, with a series of satiric vignettes of Parisian society by employing this technique. Not only was this a text with which Dickens was familiar in translation, but Asmodeus would not have been an abstruse point of reference for many of his readers: he had figured, for example, in the title of *Asmodeus in London*, a gossipy periodical of the 1830s. It was to him that Dickens referred in *Dombey and Son*, when he prayed:

> Oh for a good spirit who would take the house-tops off, with a more potent and benignant hand than the lame demon in the tale, and show a Christian people what dark shapes issue from amidst their homes, to swell the retinue of the Destroying Angel as he moves forth among them! For only one night's view of the pale phantoms rising from the scenes of our too-long neglect; and from the thick and sullen air where Vice and Fever propagate together, raining the tremendous social retributions which are ever pouring down, and ever coming thicker! (DS: 47)

The tone of this passage, and the paragraphs which surround it is wishful, conditional and, in what it implies about how things will develop should eyes remain unopened, somewhat apocalyptic. No claim is made directly that the text will fulfil an Asmodean function, but it is in certain passages in this novel, in those parts of *Bleak House* which do not belong to Esther's narrative, and in other moments of overview offered in *Little Dorrit* and *Our Mutual Friend*, that Dickens most notably organises his texts around the roof- and wall-penetrating abilities of a roving narrative viewpoint.[4]

In the previous chapter, we noted how it was in the novels of Dickens' middle period that he focused least on the life-histories and psychological traits of individuals, and favoured the exhibition of social anatomy. Here would seem to lie the roots of a complaint which in the past has been levelled against Dickens: that, to quote E.M. Forster's pernicious phrase, 'Dickens' people are nearly all flat'.[5] But such criticism (and its corollary, praise for those later novels where can be seen a 'development' in the psychological realism with which the personae are portrayed) depends on an unjustified assumption: that Dickens was, or should have been, and that we should be, relentlessly more interested in individuals than in society as a whole and its functioning. Attempts have been made to excuse or explain Dickens to some extent, by pointing to the closeness of some of his protagonists to stage and print-shop types, and there is a certain value in this emphasis, since it draws attention to his intimacy with popular culture. But I believe that he is a writer in whose case it becomes misleading to dwell for long on his virtues and deficiencies of character depiction. Here we can borrow some of the narrative theory of A.J. Greimas, who renames what we are in the habit of calling 'characters' *actants*, inviting us to think not so much about who or what they *are*, but rather, to think about what they *do*. By this, I do not mean their daily occupations, or their specific actions of marrying or murdering, but their function within the narrative.

These functions are various. First, at a fundamental level, the *actants* are caught up in dramas which draw attention to major abstract issues—desire, communication, struggle—in and around which, whether expressed or supressed, social patterns, norms, expectations and deviations are articulated.[6] Secondly, the *actants* affect our own pattern of reading: they can make us laugh, or pause, or weep. As can be seen in the case of Little Nell, these effects may differ according to prevalent cultural norms. Thirdly, and most relevantly for my immediate argument, these *actants* can highlight certain specific elements both of the society of which they are imagined to be part, and of the narrative means used to describe it. In other words, it is dangerous to speak of Dickens' 'characters' or, indeed, those of any fiction, as though these constructs are, or have been, 'real people', however tempting such a process may be. Such an approach may be alien to our learnt reading habits, but it is, I believe, a helpful way to consider Dickens.

The impersonal narrator—a 'paper being'[7] whom we have already learnt not to identify automatically with Dickens himself, however close their opinions may in fact be—has, just like any of the named figures, a function (or functions) of his own. Because of his manipulation of both text and reader, he may also be spoken of as an *actant*. And these functions are hard to divorce from other social forms at first sight unconnected with the novel. In *Commissioned Spirits*, Jonathan Arac has suggested that there is a close link between the type of narrative overview adopted by Dickens, among other nineteenth-century novelists, and new techniques of inspection and social control which were being adopted by a growing interventionist bureaucracy. Dickens' methods of making sense of and organising material had analogues elsewhere:

> Even while deploring the abuses and ineffective methods of control as the court system, mocking the newly growing bureaucracy as 'Circumlocution,' and attacking the humanly destructive control exercised in factories and Benthamite schools, Dickens's narrator is not detached from the system of observation and regulation but repeats anew its action.[8]

These techniques were used, among others, by those concerned with the social problems of cities; a concern which Dickens, of course, shared. On occasion, the means of inspection were clearly visible, as with balloon flights which offered a bird's eye view of London, or the crow's nests erected by the Metropolitan Commission of Sewers on the top of St Paul's and other high points which overlooked the East End slums.[9] When Jo, in *Bleak House*, sits on Blackfriars Bridge, and gazes up 'at the great Cross on the summit of St Paul's Cathedral . . . so golden, so high up, so far out of reach' (BH: 19), the religious comment is easy to grasp: here, as throughout the novel, 'his presence testifying to the hollow sham of a professedly Christian society'.[10] Yet Dickens' readers may well have realised the importance of this edifice in terms of secular surveillance, too: as an observation point to examine precisely those areas inhabited by such as Jo.

When the state of microbiology and germ theory meant widespread ignorance about the generation and spread of cholera, it was generally believed that the disease was disseminated by atmospheric transference, its germs floating around in poisonous clouds, in the miasma which rose from foetid water. Such a theory could easily be turned into metaphor. The chapter in *Little Dorrit* where the rapid spread of Merdle's fame and financial influence is described is entitled 'The Progress of an Epidemic', and opens with the proposition that it is as difficult to contain a moral infection as it is a physical one: a point already made in Chapter 47 of *Dombey and Son*. Moreover, the effects of Merdle's suicide were as visible as those currents of heavily polluted air which were thought to contain cholera germs and, metaphorically again, could be observed in much the same way: 'a solitary watcher on the gallery above the dome of St Paul's would have perceived the night air to be laden with a heavy muttering of the name of Merdle, coupled with every form of execration' (LD: II,25). It is by analogy this position of observer, by implication above the threat of contamination from what circulates so virulently below him, which the narrator takes up; able, after his survey of the general misery, to pinpoint at will the spot on which to concentrate—the effect of the collapse on Clennam in his Counting House.

The results of such social observations as were carried out by the Metropolitan Commission of Sewers and by other such government commissions could be found recorded in reports. The contents of these were frequently discussed in the daily and periodical press, including *Household Words* and *All the Year Round*, thus reaching a wide middle-class audience. It would be a mistake to think that fiction was the only means by which this audience became aware of social abuses. From the mid-1850s, the results of investigations were increasingly presented in statistical form: How many cubic feet of space were available to each person in home or work space? How many miles of sewers were in existence? How many people were engaged in which occupations and trades? Dickens could rely on the familiarity of many among his readership with such figures. *Hard Times*, of course, is greatly concerned with attacking the application of general statistics to particular cases, and Dickens was not the only novelist to comment that tabulated information did little to stimulate the imagination. As George Eliot put it: 'Appeals founded on generalisations and statistics require', for most Victorians, 'a sympathy ready-made, a moral sentiment already in activity'.[11] Yet the way in which Dickens presents a mass of physical detail to the reader in his crowded passages of description often leaves us, without a guiding authorial hand, to make sense of apparent jumbles of houses and alleyways, furniture and fittings, as though sifting through a pile of empirical data, in a way which has something in common with the contemporary collection of the minutiae of environmental observations.

Tabulated results typified many of the nineteenth-century modes of observation: they allowed for no personal connection between observer and observed. In this, they look back to the crucial model for this way of looking at society:

the philosopher Jeremy Bentham's idea of the *Panopticon*. This was a system of prison surveillance, whereby inmates, confined to individual cells in a ring-shaped block, could be watched over by a supervisor in a central tower. The light coming into their cells from the outside wall would assure that, for the observer, their occupants were highlighted, as though on the set of a tiny theatre. But for the inmates, the watching figure would remain in shadow. The surveillance, therefore, would be permanent in its effects, it would 'induce in the inmate a state of conscious and permanent visibility that assures the automatic functioning of power'.[12] Although partly a means of theorising about the nature of power for Bentham, its principle of construction was in fact adopted in many nineteenth-century prisons, factories and asylums. Moreover, when Bentham theorised about power relations, he envisaged the system represented by the Panopticon as providing a method by which society could function efficiently; a method which extended beyond the workings of institutions which could copy it in physical terms. Power, for Bentham, could most usefully be dispersed if society was run through with, and recognised the existence of, a network of disciplinary mechanisms. It would not be able to see them in continuous operation, but would know that they could, at any time, be pressed into service.

Phrased like this, Bentham's intentions would surely have been anathema to Dickens. We have already seen the novelist's distrust of systems and bureaucracy, for social policy which suppressed the importance of the individual. But it can be argued, as Arac has done, that the way in which Dickens constructs his novels is frequently Benthamite. He puts the narrative voice in position of overviewer, able to see connections between events, or types of personality, or modes of behaviour, which are not, and could never be, apparent to the individual consciousnesses which he represents.

Dickens even hinted that he believed that he had a special aptitude for this type of vision: 'I think it is my infirmity to fancy or perceive relations in things which are not apparent generally.'[13] Although he was specifically referring to the intellectual habit which led him to use startling, animated metaphors, the comment may be extended to highlight the fact that the principle of analogy is one of the means which he uses to structure his work.[14] As we have already seen, analogy may be used to underline aspects of social forms: we have already seen this in the case of the prison metaphor in *Little Dorrit*;[15] *Our Mutual Friend* is, to a large extent, formed around the links which can be drawn between money and dust, and so on. Or the analogy may be between characters: the pairs of fathers and sons in *Barnaby Rudge*; the practitioners of various kinds of selfishness in *Martin Chuzzlewit*. Alternatively, pointers may be placed more subtly. When the Meagles family is first described in *Little Dorrit*, Pet is introduced as a 'lovely girl . . . round and fresh and dimpled and spoilt' (LD: I,2)—a sudden critical word which disturbs the picture of conventional female perfection. Later, Clennam speculates what his future might be should he decide to fall in love with her. He never discovers: Gowan conquers. But obliquely, the text provides the answer by describing Flora Finching in tellingly similar terms: 'Flora, who had been spoiled and artless long ago, was determined to be spoiled and artless now' (LD: I,13). Clennam's romantic idealisation, it is suggested, would have disintegrated into warm-hearted, but intolerable silly superficiality.

Forster, in his *Life*, noted that curious chances, the interconnectedness of apparently random things, always led Dickens to make a comment about the smallness of the world. But he, Forster, preferred to draw a wider interpretation, adopting an organic perspective on society. Forster reminds us of the moral implications of what we may take as strange accident:

> the close relation often found thus existing between things and
> persons far apart, suggests not so much the smallness of the
> world as the possible importance of the least things done to it,
> and is better explained by the grander teaching of Carlyle that
> causes and effects, connecting every man and things with every
> other, extend through all space and time.[16]

Such an explanation is clearly a secular one, and at this level,
describes very well the point which, as we saw in the last
chapter, is made by the organisation of *Bleak House* in particular. But uncertainty creeps into the narrator's confident
tone when more spiritual matters are recalled. Here, we can
see that the model of the Panopticon only takes us a certain
distance when discussing Dickens' work. Unlike the occupant
of Bentham's central tower, the novelist can be seen to query
both his authority and his powers of visibility. Dickens may
have been impatient with many forms of evangelical fervour,
and angry with the hypocrisy which organised religion could
bring out. He may not have been an assiduous active observer
of his faith throughout his life. Nevertheless, he appears to
have retained a firm belief in the existence of God. And, as he
sometimes reminds his readers, God is the traditional bearer
of powers of overview, and hence for the narrator to claim
the same powers, he hints, would be presumptuous,
trespassing on things perhaps not lawful to reveal. As one
might expect, this apprehension is conveyed most easily when
the narration is in the voice of a named protagonist, yet
additionally, this abnegation of knowledge frequently tends
to be articulated when to think too closely about the issues at
hand would significantly challenge the basis of the bourgeois
novel. Religious authority, with its concomitant aura of pious
sentimentality, provides a convenient position behind which
to hide.

When Esther, in the brickmakers' cottage, watches an 'ugly woman, very poorly clothed' come to console the recently bereaved mother, she turns away in embarrassment both in the face of private emotion, and because she is aware of the anomaly of her social position:

> I thought it very touching to see these two women, coarse and shabby and beaten, so united; to see what they could be to one another; to see how they felt for one another; how the heart of each to each was softened by the hard trials of their lives. I think the best side of such people is almost hidden from us. What the poor are to the poor is little known, excepting to themselves and GOD. (BH: 8)

The tone of this is, in fact, unclear. From one point of view, it once more reinforces Esther's limited vision of things: what may be hidden from her is available to the more widely seeing narrator of other parts of the text. On the other hand, there *is* no moment in the book (scarcely, indeed, in Dickens' work) where we do see how mutual support among the extreme poor works in operation. Those with little to spare may offer hospitality to the suddenly destitute, as do the Nubbles to Nell and her grandfather; useful sums of money cross southern England in *Martin Chuzzlewit* from warm hearts to deserving recipients. Yet hierarchical patterns quickly spring up, even without conscious design on the part of the protagonists. Maggy's mental retardation ensures that there is an element of patronage in Little Dorrit's relationship with her, which mirrors what happens between other individuals in cases where the financial and social discrepancy is much greater. Nor is need a guarantee of help. Nell's reception, as she knocks on doors of the 'wretched hovels' on the outskirts of the industrial city, shocks both her and the reader:

> 'Do you see that?' returned the man hoarsely, pointing to a kind

of bundle on the ground. 'That's a dead child. I and five hundred other men were thrown out of work three months ago. That is my third dead child, and last. Do you think I have charity to bestow, or a morsel of bread to spare?' (OCS: 45)

Comfort among the extreme poor in Dickens' fiction seems, understandably enough, to be given in emotional rather than material terms. Hence it is not just difficult to bestow on strangers, but also hard for outsiders—whether fictional characters or the narrator himself—to imagine. The way in which Esther's reflections slip into pious, solemn homily in fact closely resembles Dickens' tone in his letters to Angela Burdett-Coutts, or his sentiments about extremes of hardship and squalor which he voiced in pieces for *Household Words* and *All the Year Round*. Once again, we are reminded of how easily the narrative voice and, in this case, the uncertainties of the narrative voice, slide into her narrative. Her function here is that of permitting the topic of appalling social conditions to be introduced. The figure of Nell, in Chapter 45 of *The Old Curiosity Shop*, carries much the same function: we are not invited to be interested in her own psychological response.

Bringing in the ultimate authority, the name of God, is one means by which Dickens shows that he is not always happy about the way in which roofs may be lifted and walls walked through. Asmodeus was originally, after all, a creature of aggressive malice: an aspect which Dickens recollects in *American Notes* when he describes defamatory, scandalmongering journalism:

> dealing in round abuse and blackguard names; pulling off the roofs of private houses, as the Halting Devil did in Spain; pimping and pandering for all degrees of vicious taste, and gorging with coined lies the most vicious man. (AN: 6)

Such behaviour does, of course, violate the sanctity of family and home, precisely the institution in which (as we shall see in Chapter 6) Dickens seems to place such strong faith for its powers to withstand the threat posed by urban life. Certainly, there is no sympathy for Wegg when he repairs, each evening, to the Boffin mansion, relishing his power 'to strip the roof off the inhabiting family like the roof off a house of cards' (OMF: III,7). For, rather than god-like, taking an overview may be regarded as inhuman in a pejorative sense. This paradox can be seen in the case of the railroad in *Dombey and Son*. On the one hand, its coming allows the traveller/reader to observe human misery from a hitherto unavailable viewpoint. And the radicality of this perspective is underscored by the fact that it has its analogue at a personal level. Despite the intense grief he feels at the death of his son, when he travels by rail, Dombey is looking out, for the first time, on something of the pains of others. Yet the railroad appears to operate independently of human or godly control, and thus, simultaneously with revealing what had previously been concealed, it is a force both frightening and destructive, the

> power that forced itself upon its iron way—its own—defiant of all paths and roads, piercing through the heart of every obstacle, and dragging living creatures of all classes, ages and degrees behind it. (DS: 20)

Unease about the moral implications of his practice might have been one motive which led to Dickens, on occasion, abnegating the position of omniscient narrator. At other times, he seems to be making a point, in Carlylean fashion, about the uncertainty inherent in gathering historical evidence. When The Warren is fired in *Barnaby Rudge*:

> some of the insurgents said that . . . they heard the shrieks of women, and saw some garments fluttering in the air, as a party of

men bore away no unresisting burdens. No one could say that
this was true or false, in such an uproar. (BR: 55)

Such reportage serves too to build up narrative suspense
about the fate of the Warren's occupants. Sometimes, this
technique of uncertainty, as when describing Miss Flite in
Bleak House, underlines a character's isolation. Not even the
narrator is by their side as a close friend, a sharer of secrets:
'Some say she really is, or was, a party to a suit, but no one
knows for certain, because no one cares' (BH: 1). In *The
Reader in the Dickens World*, Susan Horton has drawn
attention to the rhetorical use of 'seems' and 'if' in Dickens'
writing. Sometimes the 'seemses' are products of Dickens'
construction of mysteries when we do not yet know whether
'seeming may be false or true' (ED: 23). Thus we are told by
Esther, for example, that 'there seemed to be such
undisturbed repose' at Chesney Wold (BH: 18) before we or
she know more about Lady Dedlock's state of mind. At other
times, the 'ifs' may reveal that Dickens is 'feeling unsure or
unclear as to exactly what attitude to hold towards a
particular social problem';[17] or these 'ifs' may highlight the
possibilities of choice in human action, either in the future or
the past. One could cite Clennam wondering what would
happen 'if [I] had the weakness to fall in love with Pet' (LD: I,
17); or Pip, realising how poorly he has treated Joe, crying
bitterly and musing, 'If I had cried before, I should have had
Joe with me then . . . . If I could have settled down, and
been but half as fond of the forge as I was when I was little, I
know it would have been much better for me' (GE: 17).

As we have seen, despite the promise which Dickens
sometimes holds out, of being able to lay bare the secrets
enclosed in the darkly-clustered houses, or deep in human
hearts, he does not speak with a constant, confident, all-
knowing voice. The uncertainty which he betrays at times in
the task of the narrator leads back to the fact noticed at the

conclusion of the previous chapter: that if we consider the resolution of the strands of the complicated plots, far too much escapes from the edges of their apparent neatness for us to regard them as anything other than artificial. They are consoling artifices. Like the idea of an omniscient narrator, they imply a knowable society. Like Dickens in his Asmodeus role and voice asking, 'What connection can there be?', they emphasise, above all, the importance of human connections.

Dickens clearly knew how individuals could get swallowed by the mass. This can be seen both in terms of urban alienation, and when it comes to avoiding responsibility by sheltering behind the protection of a bureaucratic organisation. 'Nobody's Fault' was his original projected title for *Little Dorrit*: 'Nobody', 'the great irresponsible, guilty, wicked, blind giant of this time',[18] functions as a descriptive term for the anonymity of powerful systems, whether these are openly institutionalised, like the Circumlocution Office, or, like Rumour, operate at a deeper, ideological level. And it is no good just pointing to Dickens' observation of the operation of systems, to his concern with how power was wielded, organised and deferred to in his contemporary society without considering (as Dickens never does explicitly) what these systems most conspicuously served: the larger, increasingly organised, intensive and coordinated system of industrial capitalism.

But this was not a note on which Dickens wished to dwell. In the stress he placed on personal relations, he seems to be asserting a belief in the potential strength, as well as the responsibility, of the individual, of Somebody. He wishes to give the lie to the suspicion that there is 'left remaining no other nexus between man and man than naked self-interest, than callous "cash payment"'.[19] Like Little Dorrit and Clennam re-entering the 'roaring streets' together, 'inseparable and blessed', the urban environment is easier to cope with in shared, congenial company which promises a safe emotional centre as a bastion against the 'usual uproar' and confusion of the city (LD: II,34). Similarly, an author who claims to be able to know and show everything would be a comforting companion for the reader. But Dickens cannot sustain this role, any more than a couple of his characters can smooth out the threatening energies released by society as a whole. For like many mid-Victorian writers and thinkers, and despite the various strategies of interpretation which he tried to employ, Dickens ultimately did not know how to describe, analyse, and above all understand the material and philo-sophical complexities of his society without becoming deeply disquieted by what he observed, and without manifesting considerable uncertainty about the possibility of arriving at any solutions to the muddle, as we shall see in the next chapter. It is in his mode of narration, alternately certain and unsure, as much as in comments made directly in the narrative voice, that this disquiet is passed on to the reader.

5

Dickens and Social Change

In his novels, Dickens did not just choose to record contemporary society, giving, simultaneously, some understanding of its workings, and of the interdependence of its parts. As we have already noticed in passing, it was his expressed wish to change those of its aspects which most pained or displeased him, and he retained a belief that fiction, because of its power to reach the imagination and emotions of many people, could be an effective instrument of this change. This chapter will examine how the idea of social change is constructed in Dickens' writings, and will look at the grounds on which he bases his appeals. It is, unsurprisingly, an area of Dickens studies which has already benefited from much excellent scholarship and analysis, but this does nothing to lessen the problems, the tensions which are set up between Dickens' observation of the world around him, and the transmission of these observations into fictional form.

I

In Dickens' writing stress continually falls on two points: the importance of the present, and the importance of action. Stagnation and complacency are condemned. The ruinous, poverty-stricken and decaying Italian towns which he visited stirred up the worst of pessimistic thoughts in him: 'That there is nothing, anywhere, to be done, or needing to be done. That there is no more human progress, motion, effort, or advancement, of any kind beyond this' (Pfl, p.317). But this is not a state of mind to fall into. Those people who try to 'stop the clock of busy existence' (LD: 29) are usually presented as badly at fault: Mrs Clennam, whose repression of Arthur as a child has now been turned into a repression of herself, practises self-immolation in her room; Miss Havisham is incarcerated with the spidery wreck of her wedding cake and is determined to bring up Estella as an instrument of vengeance upon men. At best, those who shut out the present and live in the past are used to evoke the reader's compassion. Flora Finching has only her old paces to go through when she meets her former suitor. She repeats 'all the old performances—now when the stage was dusty, when the scenery was faded . . . when the lights were out' (LD: I,13).

Such past-inhabiting creatures clearly fascinated Dickens. They offer a gift to those biographically-minded critics dedicated to tracing the writer's own apprehension at dwelling too much in 'The never to be forgotten misery of that old time'.[1] But I believe that this fascination has a wider context, that of Dickens' developing concern—historical as well as personal—with the process of cause and effect, and of his emphatic, repeated conviction that the past, whether at an individual or a national level, is something to be learnt from—neither dwelt in, nor abandoned. This is precisely the lesson taught by A Christmas Carol, where the misanthropic

Scrooge, is confronted with his personal history and, in fairy-tale fashion, reforms. As Forster put it, Dickens

> was to try and convert Society, as he had converted Scrooge, by showing that its happiness rested on the same foundations as those of the individual, which are mercy and charity not less than justice.[2]

Compared with some of Dickens' characters, Scrooge, inhabiting a somewhat fantastical story world, was lucky. The man who lies dying at the end of *Mrs Lirriper's Legacy*, who 'looked back upon the green Past beyond the time when he had covered it with ashes', has no such possibility of miraculous, authorially-manipulated conversion. Mrs Clennam makes her resolute, wild dash to the Marshalsea at the end of *Little Dorrit*, to reveal to Amy the crucial circumstances concerning Arthur's past but, still determined in her uncompassionate role as the 'instrument of severity against sin', it is her fate to spend the last three years of her life a 'statue', paralysed from a stroke. Dickens uses the irredeemable nature of the past to stress the necessity of acting for the best in the present moment. One must not be like Gradgrind, who, discussing Bounderby's marriage proposal with his daughter, lets slip the 'wavering moment' when he could have got to know her better, and perhaps averted family tragedy, but 'the moment shot away into the plumbless depths of the past, to mingle with all the lost opportunities that are drowned there' (HT: I,15).

The attitudes which Dickens would have an individual adopt towards his or her past can be transposed to a wider scale. His writings, particularly the earlier ones, are not without desirably sentimental associations with earlier times. In *The Old Curiosity Shop*, the narrator rather piously claims that the ancient Gothic setting where Nell dies arouses 'that solemn feeling with which we contemplate the work of ages that have become but drops of water in the great ocean of eternity' (OCS; 52). Dickens finally returns to a similarly hallowed ecclesiastical atmosphere in *Edwin Drood*. But such examples rather give fuel to Ruskin's claim that Dickens was 'a pure modernist—a leader of the steam-whistle party *par excellence* and he had no understanding of any power of antiquity except a sort of jackdaw sentiment for cathedral towers.'[3] For Dickens was suspicious of a nostalgic attitude which held that the English past represented an idyllic world to which it would be bliss to return. He knew that such associations could easily be adopted for hypocritical ends: one neither likes nor trusts the rack-renting Casby more because he has pictures on his walls suggestive of a pastoral childhood (LD: I,13). When Dickens himself looked back he saw cruelty and oppression. In *Great Expectations*, he returned unfavourably to the society of his childhood, when legalised violence was made even more conspicuous than at the present time. Pip, on his first day in London, finding himself outside Newgate Prison, is easy game for somebody showing it off as a tourist attraction, 'where the gallows was kept, and also where people were publicly whipped, and then he showed me the Debtors' Door, out of which culprits came to be hanged'. Even with his knowledge of the rotting prison hulks, the young countryman felt that 'This was horrible, and gave me a sickening idea of London' (GE: 20). A set of false-backed books in his library at Gad's Hill were entitled 'The Wisdom of our Ancestors - I. Ignorance. II. Superstitions. III. The Block. IV. The Stake. V. The Rack. VI. Dirt. VII. Disease.' Nor was Dickens willing to swallow other myths. The American Eden in which the young Martin Chuzzlewit and Mark Tapley hope to establish themselves is no fertile Paradise but an unhealthy swamp: as much a comment on the unpropitious conditions for the origins of species, as an ironic dig at transatlantic land speculators. In his article 'The Noble Savage', Dickens throughout shows himself in little sympathy with the original inhabitants of this new-found land and with what they represented:

> Him calling rum fire-water, and me a pale face, wholly fail to reconcile me to him. I don't care what he calls me. I call him a savage, and I call a savage a something highly desirable to be civilised off the face of the earth.[4]

The Rousseauesque dream of original innocence, consolidated by the English Romantic writers, held little appeal for Dickens.

In his two most explicitly historical fictions, *Barnaby Rudge* and *A Tale of Two Cities*, Dickens draws on the past not for nostalgia, but for the lessons it can teach the present. Through a set of formal antitheses, he suggests, in the very first paragraph of *A Tale of Two Cities*, that this is a major motivation for writing the novel:

> It was the best of times, it was the worst of times, it was the age of wisdom, it was the age of foolishness . . . it was the spring of hope, it was the winter of despair . . . in short, the period was so far like the present period . . . (TTC: 1)

The work was composed with Thomas Carlyle's *The French Revolution* (1837–48) very much in mind. Dickens maintained that his preparations included re-reading this work nine times. In his preface to the first edition, he claims to envisage it as a partner to the non-fictional study. Carlyle suggested books that Dickens might consult, and read much of the novel before publication. The two differed somewhat in their interpretation of events. Carlyle was more willing to attribute the Revolution to a kind of spiritual apathy than to direct forms of social injustice, describing how 'hollow languor and vacuity is the lot of the Upper, and want and stagnation of the Lower.'[5] Dickens placed much more stress on the consequences of the terrible lack of responsibility shown by the aristocracy, developing his theory of causation and effect—the Revolution, for him, was the inevitable result of a certain combination of events and circumstances. Yet both Carlyle and Dickens agreed that the Revolution, and the causes from which it sprang, provided a warning to contemporary society. Though neither wished for such an upheaval in their own country, they could not dismiss it as a possibility. Dickens summed up his simple theory of history in the final chapter of the novel:

> Crush humanity out of shape once more, under similar hammers, and it will twist itself into the same tortured forms. Sow the same seed of rapacious licence and oppression over again, and it will surely yield the same fruit according to its kind. (TTC: 3,15)

If certain paths are taken or ignored, in other words, other events will inevitably follow. Dickens is here writing prescriptive fiction, in which he hints that his readers have the power to determine the course of events. Of course, there are passages where the narrative voice, or the characters, seem to express a belief in a providentially arranged, beatific future. Sidney Carton foresees not just the abolition of current oppression, but

> a beautiful city and a brilliant people rising from this abyss, and, in their struggles to be truly free, in their triumphs and defeats, . . . the evil of this time . . . gradually making expiation for itself and working out (TTC: 3,15)

And, in another context, Dickens, discussing *Bleak House* with Forster, described the novel as though a sombre, inexorable force lay behind the events, establishing an organic unity where 'everything tends to the catastrophe' and which works on the characters, 'drawing them on insensibly, but very certainly, to the issues that await them'.[6] He creates the impression (or illusion) that his own power of choice as a writer is as much under this fatal pull as are the figures and actions he invents. But in general, as at the end of A *Tale of Two Cities*, Dickens stresses the process of cause and effect. This is an important emphasis, for it suggests that there is a sphere of action and responsibility where decisions made by individuals carry weight.

Barnaby Rudge, the earlier of the two historical novels, perhaps had more specific links with 'the present period' than did A *Tale of Two Cities*. The anti-Catholic activities of the newly-formed Protestant Association had raised fears that No Popery might be heard loudly again, bringing violence with it. But more broadly, in describing the wild and uncontrollable mob, it played on popular apprehension fed by the Poor Law riots, and, more especially, by sporadic Chartist uprisings in the industrial North. Moreover, the ostensibly religious theme of the novel's action could be linked to the political preoccupations of the early 1840s, since much of the organisation of Chartist branches, including the payment of weekly dues and the holding of mass meetings, had been directly taken over from nonconformist practices.[7]

It has been something of a commonplace to point to the dual currents of sympathy which flow within the novel— 'Everyone knows now that unconsciously he identified himself with the rioters who burned Newgate.'[8] On the one hand, Dickens condemns the infectious thoughtlessness of violence; on the other, there is a kind of glee on his part at the energy unleashed in the rapidly paced, crowded prose of the riot scenes. Yet, in the long run, the novel comes down firmly on the side of established authority.

The rioters are damned not just by their narrowminded destructiveness, but by their retrogressive motives. Sam Tappertit recalls the life which apprentices used to lead: they in times gone by, had frequent holidays of right, broken people's heads by scores, defied their masters, nay, even achieved some glorious murders in the streets, which privileges had gradually been wrested from them . . . the degrading checks imposed on them were unquestionably attributable to the innovating spirit of the times, and . . . they united therefore to resist all change, except such change as would restore those good old English customs. (BR: 8)

As for Dennis, his fellow insurgent, what we know of Dickens' abhorrence of publicly administered punishment reinforces the irony with which he describes his occupation as hangman: 'sound, Protestant, constitutional English work' (BR: 37) committed to 'the great main object of preserving the Old Bailey in all its purity, and the gallows in all its pristine usefulness and moral grandeur' (BR: 70). As Steven Marcus has pointed out, there is a certain topicality in the way in which these rioters' attitudes are presented, since the English popular radical protest of the time tended to rest its case on what it considered to be infringements of past liberties. The manifesto of the 1839 Chartist Convention expressed just such a view of the past: 'The principles of our Charter were the laws and customs of our ancestors, under which property was secure and the working people happy and contented.'[9]

It was not that Dickens failed to sympathise with those whom society treated unfairly. But he was appalled by the translation of grievances into mass violence. Such a reaction was not peculiar to Dickens. It is a recurrent theme in those contemporary novels which treated the problems of industrial towns: the striking workers who murmur angrily with a 'savage satisfaction' outside Thornton's house in Elizabeth Gaskell's *North and South* (1854-5); the ferocious rioters who attack Mowbray Castle at the end of Disraeli's *Sybil* (1845); the 'famished and furious mass of the Operative

Class' who stone Robert Moore's mill in Charlotte Brontë's *Shirley* (1849).[10] In non-fictional theory, Dickens could state clearly and with sympathy what he understood to characterise the French Revolution:

> It was a struggle on the part of the people for social recognition and existence. It was a struggle for vengeance against intolerable oppression . . . which in its contempt of all humanity, decency, and natural rights, and in its systematic degradation of the people, had trained them to be the demons that they showed themselves, when they rose up and cast it down for ever. (MP: 133)[11]

When he dramatises the revolution into fiction the oppression is still set forward, but it is in the role of demons rather than sufferers that the revolutionaries are most strongly portrayed. They are characterised by 'their frenzied eyes;—eyes which any unbrutalised beholder would have given twenty years of his life, to petrify with a well-directed gun' (TTC: 3,2).

II

Dickens' novels clearly express ambivalent attitudes towards those who, in the past, had wished to change things. Standing still or, worse still, retrogression are presented as highly undesirable. But the dramatisation of those who go about trying to change things the *wrong* way is both more alluring in the literary opportunities which it offers, and requires less effort of analytical imagination than putting forward favourable modes of change. This is particularly apparent when Dickens moves to the problems of his own time. Here, moreover, he seems to be caught between two competing social theories, both of which are present but neither of which is dominant within his work. The one asserts that people are products of their environment, of their education.

It is a belief closely linked to an acknowledgement of the entrapping power of the past. Yet the other theory which Dickens' fiction tries to demonstrate is that change is not only possible, but that it can take place within an individual, and that wider social change may well have its most profitable source in the stimulation of individual sympathy and will to action. This can only be possible if human qualities are something innate, can be acted upon, and are independent of environmental determination.

As Raymond Williams has pointed out in his essay 'The Reader in *Hard Times*', these two incompatible ideological positions can be related to different intellectual and social strands. The former views were those argued by the rationalist philosophers Godwin and Owen; the latter were those held by many Christians. Williams goes on to note that both positions are powerfully present in *Hard Times*. 'The Godwinian version of a shaping environment, in family and very specifically in education, is there from the beginning in the Gradgrind philosophy and M'Choakumchild's school.'[12] The fact that environment can determine a whole community is suggested by the fact that we move from the streets being 'all very like one another' to the people being 'equally like another'. On the other hand, Stephen Blackpool and Rachael seem, somehow, to have survived unscathed from their systemic surroundings. Moreover, it is not sufficient to shrug one's shoulders when reading and suggest that this apparent incompatibility can be summed up by Blackpool's phrase, that it's 'aw a muddle'. For the novel doesn't just present confused, conflicting ideals, suggesting that 'life' is like this. It attempts answers, and

> great stress is laid on both ways out of the situation: the loving way of Sissy Jupe, the way reached by Louisa and even, in part, by Gradgrind, the way of suffering of Rachael—'heart' and the 'change of heart'; but also the way of a reformed educational

system, teaching 'fancy' as well as 'fact', and of a reformed economic and social system, moving beyond self-interest to mutual duty and community.[13]

At its most clearcut in *Hard Times*, this duality is found throughout Dickens' novels. It meshes with further contradictions—for example Dickens' belief, at times, that there is a social system (or systems) in need of reformation; and the dislike of systems which we have already noted his novels manifesting. It is a form of ideological uncertainty which leaves the reader perplexed. For the tone of the texts, the modes of address, seem to be prodding the Victorian addressees not just to response, but into action. Yet what responses, and what actions, do the novels, ask of them?

Dickens was credited by his contemporaries with being the writer who, before all others, enabled and stimulated a kind of sympathetic literary voyeurism towards the lives of the poor and the London poor in particular. It was due to him, commented Harriet Beecher Stowe, visiting England in 1853, that 'Fashionable literature now arrays itself on the side of the working classes.'[14] Later, in 1862, Margaret Oliphant surveyed recent English literature in the pages of *Blackwood's Edinburgh Magazine*:

> Mr Dickens was one of the first popular writers who brought pictures of what is called common life into fashion. It is he who has been mainly instrumental in leading the present generation of authors to disregard to a great extent the pictorial advantages of life on the upper levels of society, and to find a counterpicturesqueness in the experiences of the poor . . . He has made washerwomen as interesting as duchesses.[15]

Dickens took an active part in certain causes concerned with the amelioration of social conditions, and was publicly seen, and known to be active in such campaigns. Notably, as we shall see in Chapter 6, he was associated with Angela Burdett-Coutts's Urania Cottage, the home she established with the intention of reforming prostitutes, and with her plans for a model housing project in Nova Scotia Gardens, one of the most notorious areas of Bethnal Green.[16] He used his journalism to publicise specific abuses, such as the conditions which led to the deaths of 159 children from cholera in the Tooting workhouse.[17] His brother-in-law, Henry Austin, was general secretary of the Board of Health. Dickens was in regular correspondence with him and the pioneering health and sanitation reformer, Edwin Chadwick. In 1846, Dickens wrote to Lord Morpeth in the hope of obtaining some public employment or commissionership in this field—a fact which provides a check to easy generalisations about his distrust of public bodies:

> On any questions connected with the Education of the People, the elevation of their character, the improvement of their dwellings, their greater protection against disease and vice—or with the treatment of Criminals, or the administration of Prison Discipline, which I have long observed closely—I think I could do good service, and I am sure I should enter with my whole heart.[18]

Nothing came of this request, but Dickens' desire to have a magazine of his own was to a large degree prompted by his wish to see a forum where these issues could be put before a wide public.

In his earlier writings, as we have seen, Dickens highlighted particular issues: the Sabbath bills in *Sunday Under Three Heads*; the poverty and despair which drive people to alcoholism in 'Gin Shops' in *Sketches by Boz*; debtors' prisons in *Pickwick Papers*; and the notorious Yorkshire schools in *Nicholas Nickleby*. That is not to say that, in this earlier fiction, he did not occasionally glance sideways at the wider implications of the existence of specific malpractices. In *Nicholas Nickleby*, to take perhaps the most outstanding example, Nicholas, pacing the streets, despondent with personal troubles, tries to put these problems into their true perspective, reflecting, among other things,

> how in seeking, not a luxurious and splendid life, but the bare means of a most wretched and inadequate subsistence, there were women and children in that one town, divided into classes, numbered and estimated as regularly as the noble families and folks of great degree, and reared from infancy to drive most criminal and dreadful trades—how ignorance was punished and never taught—how jail door gaped, and gallows loomed for thousands urged towards them by circumstances darkly curtaining their very cradles' heads, and but for which they might have earned their honest bread and lived in peace—how many died in soul, and had no chance of life ... when he thought of all this, and selected from the mass the one slight case on which his thoughts were bent, he felt indeed that there was little ground for hope, and little cause or reason why it should not form an atom in the huge aggregate of distress and sorrow, and add one small and unimportant unit to swell the great amount. (NN: 53)

But it is precisely in opposition to seeing human conditions and social problems in terms of units and amounts that Dickens puts forward, throughout his novels, the possibility and desirability of individual effort, benevolence and charity.

According to Forster, it was in the 1840s that the notion of individual regeneration came to lodge firmly in Dickens' fiction. This was a time when 'the hopelessness of any true solution of either political or social problems by the ordinary Downing-street methods' was startlingly impressed upon him by Carlyle's writings, as well as by his own observations, with the result that he began to try to 'convert society' by showing that its happiness rested on 'the same foundations as those of the individual, which are mercy and charity no less than justice'.[19] Dickens' attitude did not change significantly in subsequent years. Moreover, as his speeches, and as such studies as Philip Collins' *Dickens and Crime* have amply shown, his belief in the need to maintain the class system as it was became, at least in his overt pronouncements, increasingly entrenched. What angered him most (as we saw in Chapter 1), was a lack of acceptance of mutual responsibility among its constituent parts. Any such acceptance cannot be legislated for; it must, for Dickens, take place at an individual level and, like all the best reform, radiate outwards. However powerful his writing might have been at pointing to abuses, he offers no radical surgery.

One reason for this is a simple one. Indivisible from Dickens' support for the existing class structure—a structure which did, as he saw it, allow for individual activity and economic enterprise—was the fact that although Dickens might attack the working and living conditions to which industrialism could give rise, he did not come out against the growth and development of manufacturing industry *per se*. He was no Luddite, no Ruskin, prophesying in 1859 a nightmare vision of the twentieth century, with

> the whole of the island . . . set as thick with chimneys as the masts stand in the docks of Liverpool; that there shall be no meadows in it; no trees; no gardens; only a little corn grown upon the house tops, reaped and thrashed by steam; that you do not even have room for roads, but travel either over the roofs of your mills, on viaducts; or under their floors, in tunnels; that, the smoke having rendered the light of the sun unserviceable, you work always by the light of your own gas: that no acre of English ground shall be without its shaft and its engine.[20]

Nor—despite the claims made for him by F.R. and Q.D. Leavis in the essay on *Hard Times* in *The Great Tradition* (1948) and in *Dickens the Novelist* (1970)—was he some nineteenth-century Lawrentian prototype demanding, as does that writer at the end of his essay 'Nottingham and the Mining Country', 'Do away with it all, then, ... Pull down my native village to the last brick ... Make a new England.'[21] Indeed, in a speech of 1865, Dickens listed Luddite actions in a long summary of the social evils which had afflicted the country in relatively recent times, but which now, happily, had disappeared: he spoke against 'the destruction of machinery which was destined to supply unborn millions with employment'.[22] In fact, he heartily approved of much to do with the operation and consequences of industrialisation. He may, of course, have been flattering his Birmingham audience when he talked of

> the name and fame of its capitalists and working men; ... the greatness and importance of its merchants and manufacturers; ... its inventions, which are constantly in progress; ... the skill and intelligence of its artisans which are daily developing; and the increased knowledge of all portions of the community.[23]

But this does not represent an isolated example. In the very years he composed *Hard Times*, he wrote excitedly that

> the factory itself is certainly not a 'thing of beauty' in its externals. But it is a grand machine in its organisation—the men, the fingers, and the iron and steel, all work together for one common end.[24]

The pages of *Household Words* and *All the Year Round* demonstrate a fascination with industrial processes. In articles commissioned from others, written in collaboration with them, or entirely by himself, we can learn of making glass or refining gold (though these pieces could not be said of course, to deal with 'heavy' industry).

Ruskin, in the same letter of 1870 in which he called

Dickens 'a pure modernist', claimed that 'His hero is essentially the ironmaster'.[25] Very probably he had in mind the presentation of Rouncewell in *Bleak House*, and the description there of a productive working town dominated by a good employer, rather on the pattern of the American manufactories about which Dickens commented so enthusiastically in *American Notes*. In Rouncewell's son, Watt, there is some indication of where the future of England must lie, for Rouncewell, unlike the sterile Sir Leicester, *has* a son. Moreover, this son's name links him both to industrialism—to the enterprising nature of one of Samuel Smiles' self-made men, James Watt—and also to Wat Tyler, leader of the Peasants' Revolt, symbol for Sir Leicester of everything which most threatened the predominance of his class, and one whom Dickens, in *A Child's History of England*, had called 'a hard-working man who had suffered much ... a man of a much higher nature and a much braver spirit, than any of the parasites who exulted then or have exulted since over his defeat'. (CHE: 19).

But it should be stressed that Rouncewell was an *ironmaster*, a member of a profession which had a very good reputation as employers, just as cotton millowners had a very bad one. Dickens was well aware of this distinction which he helped to maintain. When he visited the already notorious Manchester in 1838, he claimed in a letter that

I saw the *worst* cotton mill. And then I saw the *best* ... There was no great difference between them ... So far as seeing goes, I have seen enough for my purpose, and what I have seen has disgusted and astonished me beyond all measure. I mean to strike the heaviest blow in my power for these unfortunate creatures.[26]

The absolute truth of this is debatable. One could query whether Dickens, becoming well known as a publicist, would indeed have obtained entry into the *worst* cotton mill.[27] But more striking is the way in which Dickens, who certainly had opportunities to attack the abuses of the factory system, both in and out of fiction, during the next decades, consistently failed to come up with the goods—a delaying process which is well documented by Philip Collins in his article on 'Dickens and Industrialism'.[28] He might have looked at, say, the topical controversy and legislation proposals concerning factory children. He glances at this obliquely in *Nicholas Nickleby* when, foreshadowing *Hard Times*, he constrasts the lives of gipsy children at Hampton with those which are spent 'in the midst of dreadful engines which make young children old before they know what childhood is' (NN: 50). But rather than look at such a subject in any specific detail, he retreated in his next novel, *The Old Curiosity Shop*, to describing the Midlands industrial area in highly self-consciously literary terms. He translated what he himself had observed on his 1838 journey from Birmingham to Wolverhampton (in a letter, he commented that 'such a mass of dirt and gloom and misery ... I never before witnessed'[29]) into a compositional exercise which emphasises the sensationalised horror of it all. In daytime could be seen, on every side, 'tall chimneys, crowding in on each other, and presenting that endless repetition of the same, ugly form which is the horror of oppressive dreams'; mounds of ashes, collapsing and doorless houses, machines which are at once 'tortured creatures' and untamed, 'wrathful monsters', everything covered in the dense dark cloud, the 'black vomit' which comes blasting out of the smokestacks. But it is the hellish night-time which seized Dickens' imagination most strongly:

> night-time, when the smoke was changed to fire, when every chimney spirted up its flame; and places, that had been dark vaults all day, now shone red-hot, with figures moving to and fro within their blazing jaws, and calling to one another with hoarse cries—night, when the noise of every strange machine was

aggravated by the darkness; when the people near them looked wilder and more savage; when bands of unemployed labourers paraded the roads, or clustered by torch-light round their leaders, who told them, in stern language, of their wrongs, and urged them on to frightful cries and threats; when maddened men, armed with swords and firebrand, spurning the tears and prayers of women who would restrain them, rushed forth on errands of terror and destruction, to work no ruin half so surely as their own. (OCS: 45)

This vision betrays, once again, fear of the masses and, simultaneously, distances them, controls them and their energies by turning them into prose which, in its biblically styled rhetoric, uses them as a subject for a virtuoso display of writing. The sweeping cadence becomes slightly more sympathetic in tone as it continues, drawing our attention to the pitifulness of orphans and widows, but Dickens, in this novel, never pauses to look beneath the apocalyptic surface, never considers what causes the unemployment that drives the men to desperation and angry violence.

Yet when Dickens ceases to write in an apocalyptic style, and combines his verbal energy with circumstantial detail, it becomes hard to pin down the direction of his sympathies. In particular, the conflict between the priorities and rights of class and individual can be seen as unresolved. *The Chimes* provides an interesting example of this. This was the first of Dickens' fictions to present sustained, general social protest. Coming out in December 1844, it was the direct Christmas follow-up to *A Christmas Carol*. It was an immediate success. Nearly 20,000 copies were sold within the next two or three months, and as many as five stage dramatisations appeared in London in the few weeks following its publication. It was immediately controversial, too. On the 31 December, the *Globe*'s critic remarked that 'Dicken's [sic] new work is attacked and defended with a degree of ardour which scarcely any other subject is capable of inspiring.'[30] Many, like Dickens' friend Bulwer Lytton, felt that unlike A *Christmas Carol*, it did not create 'agreeable feelings' for 'its moral is untrue and dangerous . . . the fierce tone of menace to the rich is unreasonable and ignorant.'[31] It would seem that Dickens, in writing this 'Tract for the Times', was influenced both by the angry social criticism of Carlyle in *Past and Present* (which had come out in the previous year) and by the many current newspaper reports of poverty and distress, some of which (e.g. about the eyestraining work of seamstresses, the woman who tries to drown her own child) have direct echoes in the text. Topical, too, was the attack on the hardships suffered by agricultural labourers. The corrected proofs of *The Chimes* show that Dickens changed Fern's native county from Hertfordshire to Dorsetshire; particularly apt since, as Lord Ashley warned at a Sturminster Agricultural Dinner in 1843, Dorset was becoming 'a by-word in men's mouths'.[32] A sensation had been caused by the publication, the same year, of Richard Sheridan's account of the terrible state of the Dorset peasants.

In one of the many moments of vision in the novella, this countryman, Fern, is seen speaking out at a banquet of pompous and self-righteous dignitaries. He tells how he is jailed when breaking a branch when out nutting, jailed if he eats a rotten apple or turnip. He demands 'in mercy, better homes when we're a-lying in our cradles'. The leisured classes may come and draw the picturesqueness of their tumbledown cottages, but he demands that they look at the realities of country life instead. Finally, he asks:

Give us better food when we're a working for our lives; give us kinder laws to bring us back when we're a going wrong; and don't set Jail, Jail, Jail, afore us, everywhere we turn. There an't a condescension you can show the Labourer then, that he won't take, as ready and as grateful as a man can be; for he has a patient,

peaceful, willing heart. But you must put his rightful spirit in him
first ... (TC: 3rd Quarter)

As well as noting the topicality of the story, we must keep in
mind the way in which Dickens, in his sympathetic
presentation of this labouring man, does not actually
challenge the class position of his protagonists—only the use,
or misuse, which those with power and money make of this
position. Fern, almost as though he had been reading Carlyle
and sharing his conclusions, demands increased paternalism,
claims that he will meet condescension with readiness and
gratitude. As the passage quoted above shows, Dickens
betrays no trace of irony in narrating this. Indeed, as Sheila
Smith has demonstrated, it very much parallels Dickens'
attitudes outside his fiction, as shown towards John Overs, a
carpenter who corresponded with him about Carlyle's
Chartism, and whom the novelist encouraged until he
manifested signs of ideas and ambitions which Dickens
considered to be above his station.[33] The same theme of the
poor gratefully acknowledging the attention of the rich is
presented approvingly in *Oliver Twist*—Oliver, snatched back
from Mr Brownlow's by the thieves, is agonised that his
benefactor should think him ungrateful. In *Bleak House*, Jo,
the crossing sweeper, 'never knowd what it was all about' but
was 'wery thankful' to Allan Woodcourt for taking him out
of Tom-All-Alone's (BH: 47).

Yet if *The Chimes* was no more than a tale in praise of the
right kind of paternalism, it would hardly have stirred up
such violent reactions in Lytton and others. The dramatisation of terrible social conditions, of the total despair caused
by poverty, spoke more strongly than Fern's modulated,
unthreatening words.

Once again, it is a question of analysis, even of paying
attention to our own reactions as we read, and of noting those
of Dickens' contemporaries, revealing more than the text

appears to tell us on the surface. And a crucial area for considering the *un*said of the text comes with Dickens' incorporation of contemporary, topical detail. For, despite his unwavering compassion for the individual representatives of the poor, and despite his knowledge, however partial, of the actual living conditions of industrial Britain, Dickens often carefully selected, rearranged or even altered material when it came to his fiction. Despite the idea put forward in Chapter 2, that the same techniques of *analysis* may theoretically be used on all texts, whether they conventionally fall into the categories of fiction or non-fiction, here we have a case of a writer's *practice* unmistakably differing according to genre. Certainly, an aesthetic desire for dramatic effect partly lay behind this, but one must consider too the ideological importance of Dickens' alterations and omissions.

Hard Times is an interesting novel to consider in this respect for, as we have seen, it is a work which attempts to offer a fictional orderliness not just in terms of telling what happens to individual lives, but also through pointing to possible solutions for some of society's ills—ills, in this case, in the sphere of familial and industrial relations. In its final lines, having run through the destinies of its characters, it explicitly tries to involve the reader in making a bridge between the fictional and the material world: 'Dear reader! It rests with you and me, whether, in our two fields of action, similar things shall be or not'. (HT: 3,9). The reader, it is suggested, now shares the same privileged position as the writer even though his or her field of action is hardly as clearly determined—the one evidently must write; the other, what?

But does the reader in fact share this position? His or her viewpoint might be constructed so that it is identical to that of the narrative presentation, but not, I think, to that of the writer himself. For in turning his material into fiction, we see that Dickens has caused some interesting transformations to take place. Let us take, for example, one notable case of factual and textual omission.

Dickens was certainly not ignorant of the dangers of industrial manufactory. Indeed, in the same issue of *Household Words* in which appeared Chapters 7 and 8 of *Hard Times*, was an article by Henry Morley called 'Ground in the Mill':

> There are many ways of dying. Perhaps it is not good when a factory girl, who has not the whole spirit of play spun out of her for want of meadows, gambols upon balls of wool, a little too near the exposed machinery that is to work it up, and is immediately seized, and punished by the merciless machine that digs its shaft into her pinafore and hoists her up, tears out her left arm at the shoulder joint, breaks her right arm, and beats her on the head.

He points out, quietly, that the girl still lives. Perhaps it would have been better for her to be like

> the boy whom his stern master, the machine, caught as he stood on a stool wickedly looking out of the window at the sunlight and the flying clouds. These were no business of his, and he was fully punished when the machine he served caught him by one arm and whirled him round and round till he was thrown down dead. There is no lack of such warnings to idle boys and girls.

Morley drops his tone of bitter irony as he goes on to enumerate case after case of those who have become entangled with the machine straps when adjusting covers which have been blown across shafts, picking cotton off machinery, and have had limbs torn off, been crushed, mangled, and partly dismembered.[34]

Not only did Dickens obviously know of the material

contained in this article in his own journal, but he actually deleted a long reference, in Chapter 13, by Stephen Blackpool, to the very same type of accident having happened to Rachael's little sister 'Wi' her child arm tore off afore thy face', and to the fact that the manufacturers did not necessarily act when legislation told them to box off machinery, when

> that Government gentleman comes and make's report. Fend off the dangerous machinery, box it off, save life and limb; don't rend and tear human creatures to bits in a Chris'en country! What follers? Owners sets up their throats, cries out. 'Onreasonable! Inconvenient! Troublesome!' Gets to Secretaries o' State wi' deputations, and nothing's done.[35]

Rachael tells Stephen to let such things be, they only lead to hurt, and submissively he agrees. But the point has been made, reinforced by a footnote which had directed the reader back to the Morley article: a linking of fiction with factual reporting which constituted an unprecedented practice for Dickens. Yet by the time *Hard Times* appeared in print Dickens had chosen to edit out this reference, which was not just topical, but graphic and effective, and clearly antagonistic towards the millowners.

I would suggest that it is this last factor, combined with Dickens' continuing belief that fiction should entertain as well as instruct, which was the prime motivating force behind the deletion, as it lies behind the exclusion and full treatment of controversial material in some other cases. For the overall tendency of this novel runs against allowing facts to speak for themselves, as was the case not just in Morley's piece, but in many contributions to *Household Words* and other periodicals for which Dickens himself wrote. But in *Hard Times*, Dickens' rhetoric often forces us to smile before we protest, as when he describes the piston of the steam-engine, for example, which 'worked monotonously up and down, like the head of an elephant in a state of melancholy madness' (HT: 1,5). The metaphor draws more attention to the cleverness of the writing than to the tedium of mechanical processes.

Others of Dickens' apparently fanciful metaphors take on more alarming resonances when examined in the light of his non-fictional prose, offering us opportunities for the type of synchronic, cross-textual reading suggested in Chapter 2. There is a slightly amusing strangeness in hearing that Coketown was 'a town of unnatural red and black like the painted face of a savage' (HT: 1,5), until one turns to Dickens' hysterical attack on the 'Noble Savage', the

> howling, whistling, clucking, stamping, jumping, tearing savage ... cruel, false, thievish, murderous; addicted more or less to grease, entrails, and beastly customs; a wild animal ... a conceited, tiresome, bloodthirsty, monotonous humbug—[36]

a bloodthirsty savage not all that different, in some of these respects, from a member of the angry industrial masses as portrayed in contemporary fiction.

This raises another, and much more serious point about the fictional rhetoric of *Hard Times*. Although Dickens, perhaps disingenuously, claimed that he had no particular model in mind when describing Coketown, there is no doubt that he made extensive use of material gathered when reporting the Preston strike for *Household Words*. This article, despite its closeness to other contemporary reports of events in Preston should not, as Chapter 2 indicated, offer a yardstick of 'Truth' against which to measure fiction. Rather, it offers us an opportunity to see how Dickens placed his rhetorical emphasis differently when writing in what he considered to be two distinct modes: journalistic reportage, and fiction. In his article 'On Strike', he describes a delegates' meeting during the lock-out, emphasising, incidentally, that in Preston there was no disturbance by night or day in the streets, nor could such a disturbance be found in police records. The professional speaker, Gruffshaw, in 'full boil' with his ranting rhetoric at the meeting, is soon silenced with the full assent of those present by the persuasive hand of the chairman falling gently on his shoulder. Dickens' report deliberately emphasises the honourable character of the working man:

> Perhaps the world could not afford a more remarkable contrast than between the deliberate collected manner of these men proceeding with their business, and the clash and hurry of the engines among which their lives are passed. Their astonishing fortitude and perseverance, their high sense of honour among themselves; the extent to which they are impressed with the responsibility that is upon them of setting a careful example, and keeping their order out of any harm and loss of reputation; the noble readiness in them to help one another ... could scarcely ever be plainer to an ordinary observer of human nature.[37]

Yet in *Hard Times*, those who are explicitly credited with similar virtues, who have 'an untiring readiness to help and pity one another' (HT: 1,6) are not, for the most part, the working people, despite the feelings of Stephen and Rachael for one another, but the performers of Sleary's circus, those representatives of the only desirable form of anarchy, the world of Fancy. The roaring, pounding, fiery-faced orator, Slackbridge, is not quietly hushed by his more responsible peers, but his ranting address to 'my friends, the down-trodden operatives of Coketown ... the slaves of an iron-handed and grudging disposition', reinforced by cries of 'Good! hear, hear, hear! Hurrah!' from his enthusiastic audience, is allowed to stand as the typical delivery of a thoroughly unflattering representative of all organisers of the industrially oppressed (HT: 2,4). Our sympathy for the working man is directed to fall on one individual, Blackpool, who is sent to Coventry by this meeting for reasons which are never fully explained, thus further suggesting the irrational irresponsibility of the workers *en masse*. Stephen's employer, Bounderby, is certainly attacked in the text. But this is not because of the position which he holds within the structure of industrial capitalism. He is satirised for his ridiculous hypocrisy, his conceit, and above all because he misuses his responsibilities, and violates the trust which Stephen, as a good worker, is willing to place in him.

It is clear that Stephen becomes especially worthy of our interest not through being a representative of the masses but through having been ostracised by them. But it is his rescue, fatally injured, from the bottom of a disused mine shaft (no attention is drawn to the fact that someone must have been responsible for this environmental hazard) which fully demonstrates the role of this *actant*. He is exhibited in his dying moments as 'a poor crushed human creature' who elicits 'a low murmur of pity' from 'the throng' (HT: 3,6). This figure is used to prompt feelings of the heart, stirring Gradgrind and Louisa, already softened by personal sorrow, into more humane thoughts about the conditions of the factory workers. The scene is a theatrical appeal to sentimentality, an appeal to a change of heart on a purely individual level.

This might, at any rate, be a satisfactory summing-up of the sad scene were it not for the fact that Stephen was crushed by more than inhumane labour relations. As we just saw, he was as isolated from his working peers as from his master. He was also crushed by the divorce laws, which ensured that one of his income could never hope to be released from a deeply unsatisfactory marriage. In each case, Dickens could be said to be making a plea for the rights of the individual—only one can instantly query the nature of these rights, since they are not envisaged as existing within any radically altered class structure. From Dickens' own position, unwilling or unable to look at the problems which undeniably existed, from outside the social structuring which he wished to take as axiomatic, an appeal based on, and directed towards, the individual, was the most feasible form of challenge. But since this individual reader must live within society, formed by it as well as being a potential reformer of it, such an appeal is necessarily a complex one. Moreover, when one knows what the text has suppressed and concealed, one sees, too, on how partial a view of the workings of this structure the readers are asked to base their own future action, to carry into operation their own personal little 'change of heart', stimulated through the emotionally persuasive medium of fiction. When this partiality of view is combined with the contradictory nature of the prescriptive messages noted by Williams, we see how impossible it is to arrive at a clear, non-contradictory description of the manner in which Dickens' novels suggest that social problems of whatever nature can be tackled.

What a reading of the novels dramatises most forcibly is precisely this sense of ideological uncertainty. This uncertainty was not just peculiar to Dickens, but was representative of far more wide-reaching trends among members of a concerned, questioning, yet apprehensive Victorian middle class.

6

Disruptive Angels: Dickens and Gender

Dickens' treatment of women has had a bad press. The accusations levelled against him have been threefold: that he helped reinforce the dominant ideology that a woman's place is in the home, cheerfully supporting her husband, father or brother, and deftly supervising the running of the household; that, allied to this, his writing shows slender sympathy for women who busied themselves with public causes; and thirdly, that he either denied women their sexuality, or treated it entirely from a male angle, with a malodorous relish which vacillated between the lascivious and the coy.

Ample support can be found for all three charges, although this support is undermined by instances which show that whatever the partial truth of such generalisations, it was impossible for Dickens' writings to embody them wholesale. Similarly, although we can point to the literary typicality of Dickens' views by citing copiously from other Victorian (usually male) novelists, prose writers, periodicals, medical textbooks, and so on, the fact that a certain picture of womanhood was promoted as socially desirable is, of course, no guarantee that all women did, could, or wanted to conform to such an ideal. Moreover, the mid-nineteenth century, showing, as it did, greatly increased interest in the status of woman—as a medical subject to be examined, as a political issue, as a focus for arguments about education and employment—simultaneously problematised her.

Feminist criticism of Dickens has tended to concentrate on the simplest issue: his presentation of women as characters and, in some cases, as caricatures. But this is an area where it is useful to remind ourselves of the dangers of thinking in terms of 'character'. We saw in Chapter 3 how Esther, constructed through her own voice, slid in and out of her own narrative, and became at times a verbally passive vessel, filled by the narrator's own tones and vocabulary. If we think of the majority of Dickens' women as *actants*, to employ Greimas's terms again, we see how they, and their roles, are in fact articulated by the social structures which contain them: they take their identity from the position they occupy in relation to certain commonly held attitudes about love, marriage, motherhood, and so on. Individuality, if it exists, comes through deviance from a gender-determined norm, rather than from the woman being allowed any possibility of personal transcendence.

However, within and outside Dickens' texts, we do discover the presence of those whose deviance is so pronounced that they have the effect of denying this supposed or desired norm. We might think of Rosa Dartle, or Miss Wade, or Estella. They thus serve to disrupt the norm itself. They reveal not just the hypothetical assumptions on which it was based, but also the structuring and power relations within society which such a norm, consciously or unconsciously, was designed to serve. Moreover, once the matters of woman's sexuality and woman's role have been brought into prominence, they work to destabilise the position of the male.

Two works have become clichés in feminist exposées of mid-nineteenth-century attitudes: Ruskin's 'Of Queens' Gardens' (1865) and Coventry Patmore's *The Angel in the House* (1854–56). Patmore's poem introduces woman as God created her:

> Her disposition is devout,
> Her countenance angelical.

Towards her conquering hero, her future husband,

> Her will's indomitably bent
> On mere submissiveness to him.[1]

Ruskin, too, invests his subject with a celebratory sanctity:

> And wherever a true wife comes, this home is always round her. The stars only may be over her head, the glow-worm in the night-cold grass may be the only fire at her foot, but home is yet wherever she is; and for a noble woman it stretches far round her, better than ceiled with cedar or painted with vermilion, shedding its quiet light far, for those who else were homeless.[2]

But if these seem familiar stereotypes to us, their familiarity is no reason for them to be passed over, since they formed a central support of popular middle-class mythology. They belong to precisely the same tradition which Dickens helped to create. The Christmas Books, in particular, venerate the household gods. The Cricket, for example, extols the merits of John Peerybingle's wife, speaking of the hearth she blessed and brightened: 'the hearth which, but for her, were only a few stones and bricks and rusty bars, but which has been, through her, the Altar of your Home' (CoH: Chirp the Third). *The Angel in the House* sold better in Victorian England and America than any other poetic work apart from

Tennyson's *Idylls of the King* (1862) (which, with its portrayal of a whole society split apart by the Queen's adultery, also played its part in reinforcing sexual stereotypes). *Sesame and Lilies*, of which 'Of Queens' Gardens' forms a part, was Ruskin's most popular work: by 1905, 160,000 copies had been printed.

Idealised domesticity recurs throughout Dickens' work. In both fictional and non-fictional works, the narrative voice speaks gushingly of 'Home, and fireside peace and happiness' (OT: 29); begs young couples to 'cherish the faith that in home, and all the English virtues which the love of home engenders, [for here] lies the only true source of domestic felicity' (SB: p. 602). Yet the dialogue in *Barnaby Rudge* reveals how dangerous it is to regard family affections as axiomatic. To do this can amount to emotional blackmail. Mr Chester's arguments ring tyrannically hollow when he speaks of 'those amazingly fine feelings and those natural obligations which must subsist between father and son ... The relationship between father and son, you know, is positively quite a holy kind of bond' (BR: 12). Moreover, a reading of Dickens' works does not turn up a galaxy of believably happy families who serve to support his theoretical celebration of the household gods: the hard work necessary to create or sustain such an environment is thereby stressed. The 'jaded sullenness' of the little Gradgrinds (HT: 3); the incessant low-key sadism practised by the Smallweeds in *Bleak House*; the determined marketing for marriage by Mr and Mrs Podsnap of their understandably reluctant daughter Georgiana in *Our Mutual Friend*; the 'jealous, stony-hearted, distrustful company' that comprises the 'pleasant little family circle' of the Chuzzlewits (MC: 4) provide a complete antithesis to the delights of hearth and home. Clearly, each serves, on the surface, as a didactic example: parenthood without love and understanding is an unlovely business. But what the surface of the text does not cope with is the different type of attraction offered by these families. Instead of bland domesticity, we have the capricious variety of unpredictable tempers, the simmering possibilities for rebellion, the enjoyable voyeurism of looking into families where relatives are even more unreasonable and grotesque than our own. Not only does Dickens' fiction continually provide lively concrete examples which contradict the ideal articulated so easily in the narrative voice, not only do they call the possibility of realising these ideals somewhat into question, but they make us query whether the achievement of marital felicity is all that we, in reading, desire.

Noticeably, where domestic felicity is found, it is not restricted to the middle class, the class base of most of Dickens' readers; indeed, the note of idealisation is particularly strong when dealing with Joe and Biddy at the end of *Great Expectations* or, despite their temporary difficulties, the Plornishes in Bleeding House Yard, in *Little Dorrit*. Nor need the homely unit have a conventional membership in order to radiate peace and security: one need only think of the extended family aboard the 'bacheldore' Dan Peggoty's boat. But whatever its context, it is used to underline not just the importance played by the emotions in relationships, but also of good management, and a proper maintenance of duties, within a home. Through this, the particular value of the family, whatever its particular form, lies in its ability to function as a coherent unit against confusing, alienating, dangerous modern society.[3] The obviousness of this homiletic point for the Victorian reader perhaps explains the flat conventionality of the language when it is spelled out, for example in *Oliver Twist*: 'Bleak, dark, and piercing cold, it was a night for the well-housed and fed to draw round the bright fire and thank God they were at home' (OT: 23). When, in his non-fictional writing, this security is brought into direct juxtaposition with concrete details in the world outside it is easy to pass over its implied constraints and understand the appeal of its comfort. In 'Wapping Workhouse', Dickens contrasts: 'that young woman who is not here and never will come here; who is courted, and caressed, and loved, and has a husband, and bears children, and lives in a house' (OT: III), with the diseased, distressed inhabitants of the 'Foul wards'; the 'old ladies in a condition of feeble dignity' who shared accommodation with those prone to epileptic fits and hysteria; the unmarried mothers, and oakum-picking refractories. Until one pauses to consider how a strong insistence on the desirability of the close-knit nuclear family helps to accentuate the marginalisation of those women who are forced to take their place in a very different type of institution, the life of the courted and caressed young woman can seem an unquestionably preferable alternative.

The idea of a well-kept home and sanctuary does not necessarily imply that it contains a full family unit. There is, for example, Sol Gills' ship-shape establishment in *Dombey and Son*; the Nubbles' home in *The Old Curiosity Shop*; even the familiar, cheering welcome offered by Master Humphrey's hearth and clock. And, where angels do unfurl their wings, they do not necessarily do so within the terms of the nuclear family. Rose Maylie is one of these celestial begins:

> in the lovely bloom and spring-time of womanhood; at that age, when, if ever angels be for God's good purposes enthroned in mortal forms, they may be, without impiety, supposed to abide in such as hers ... earth seemed not her element. (OT: 29)

But though all her attributes were 'made for Home, and fireside peace and happiness', it is her half-brother, Oliver, whom we *see* her succouring, rather than observing her future married life with Harry. Ruth Pinch seems set up to bring happiness to John Westlock, yet it is on her brother Tom that

117

she practises her busy yet bashful homemaking. But in neither of these cases does the young woman continue for ever as an unwedded angel. They, like Esther in *Bleak House* or, in somewhat different circumstances, Little Dorrit, are serving a kind of house and family-keeping apprenticeship. For these tasks are, rightly, presented as no easy ones. The ability to run a home smoothly, the novels suggest, is a sign of emotional maturity. The disastrous consequences if these qualities are absent are shown when David and Dora marry. Dora's budgeting is non-existent; her ability to manage servants with a fondness for the bottle and their employers' teaspoons is lamentable; meat from apparently deformed sheep appears half raw on the table. Moreover, the manner in which she fails to fulfil housewifely duties emphasises the interdependence of gender and class. It calls out a rebuke from David, who reminds her that:

> Our want of system and management, involves not only ourselves ... but other people ... there is contagion in us ... we incur the serious responsibility of spoiling everyone who comes into our service... unless we learn to do our duty to those whom we employ, they will never learn to do their duty to us. (DC: 48)

Dora's function, at this point, is to dramatise not just the folly of being an unprepared, irresponsible homemaker, but to provide a moral warning to those young men who may be lured by empty-headed prettiness. The first-person narrative helps ensure that the reader takes David's point of view. The challenge which Dora represents to him—his powers of judgement, and, in household terms, of authority, are called into question—is subsumed by his taking on a role which simultaneously enhances his growth to maturity, and stunts hers: he reasserts his gender identity by assuming a protective, patronising paternalism. Potential conflict defused in this way, with David in command as both husband and narrator, it is small wonder that Dora is denied a position from which to speak.

Dora's antithesis is not so much Agnes, since the household responsibility which seems always to have been a feature of the latter's perfection appears inborn, 'natural', achieved through experience but without notable effort. Rather, it is Bella Wilfer, in *Our Mutual Friend*, who combines learning her new role of wife with consolidating the most important of lessons: the importance of love as against money. Happily, of course, the text ensures that her husband has provided her with highly favourable conditions for such an education: a 'clever little servant' and £150 a year. She applies herself diligently to the *Complete British Family Housewife*, the text which is to help bring out her innate womanly powers: 'having a quick wit and a fine ready instinct [she] made amazing progress in her domestic efficiency' (OMF: III,5). Reading today, it is difficult not to hear alarm bells in the way Bella's marriage is described by Dickens with apparent delight, as she sits sewing 'like a sort of dimpled little charming Dresden-china clock by the very best maker' (OMF: III,11), and through Rokesmith's voice, as 'a most precious and sweet commodity' (OMF: III,5). She herself is made to describe her first home as 'the charm-ingest of dolls' houses', a phrase impossible to read without post-Ibsen emotional claustrophobia. Yet she desires to be 'something so much worthier' than the doll within it. The resulting domestic and affectionate activity is rewarded, of course, both by the possession of a far grander establishment, tropical aviary, ivory casket of jewels and all, and, simultaneously with this extravagant gift, by a revelation of the plotting and deception in which she has become enmeshed. It is this unmasking of purpose shared by the Boffins and Rokesmith which in fact reveals the very worst aspect of Bella's subordinate role, manipulated, kept in the dark, deprived of making choices freely, by those who presume to know better than she. Similarly (although not with such a stress on moral education and, admittedly, along with Woodcourt) Esther had been manipulated in her actions and emotions by Jarndyce's paternalistic scheming.

Dora is shown to be unwilling or rather, incapable, of making any such effort as Bella does. Her insistence on being called 'child-wife' is her means of denying responsibility for these domestic shortcomings. David's taking it up, and its repeated use in the novel, allows him to cope with the error of judgement he has made. It sets Dora, both for himself and for the reader, into a specific role. It prevents her being considered as a character, both in the imaginary terms of the novel, and in our analysis of it, since it precludes the possibility of development. Dora is frozen as surely as the mentally defective Maggy in *Little Dorrit* is stuck at the age of ten; or as the relationship between Maggy's 'little mother' and Clennam must be, for the latter, until he realises that it is an adult woman he is dealing with, and starts to call her something other than the affectionate yet highly patronising 'my child'. Death—the fate of many Dickens' 'children' for whom the passage to adulthood would be problematic, either in literal terms because of their health, or in constructional terms because of the demands that it would place on the plot (Paul Dombey fits both categories)—is the only possible release which allows David, and the reader, to focus on higher things, on the angelic Agnes, forever pointing upward.

Dickens reinforces his idealised brides by presenting the other side of the coin: traditional anti-feminist stereotypes of shrewish, domineering women with the ability to reduce men to cowering subordination. Very rarely does he depict marriages which have settled, or disintegrated, into mundane routine, into catalogues of minor difficulties and constraints or hardships, where there is only neutral feeling between the partners. The nearest he comes to this is with the grumbling Tetterbys in Chapter III of *The Haunted Man*, but even this transformation of an otherwise happy family is shown to be a form of magical delusion. He seems to have found the possibilities for satire far more tempting, introducing such figures as Mrs Wilfer, head embraced in a pocket handkerchief and greeting visitors with a majestic faintness; Mrs MacStinger, in *Dombey and Son*, ferociously cleaning her house and forcing her sea captain lodger to take refuge on a dry island in the middle of the floor; or, for that matter, the garrulous, sentimental types, whether Mrs Nickleby or Mrs Gamp, the latter drawing continual humour out of the traditional feminine spheres of bringing people into and out of the world. They are presented with the same energetic awfulness as many of Dickens' less savoury male characters, but unlike these, they fall very readily into a familiar cultural tradition, from Noah's wife in the Mystery plays to television situation comedy. We find ourselves laughing at learned residual responses to an anti-feminist tradition, as well as at the individualistic inventiveness which is also part of their presentation.

But the question which we must ask of the novels is this: if a woman's 'natural', instinctive bent is towards homemaking, towards maintaining a comfortable family environment, how did these personae come to be as they are? We see the end-product, not the process of frustration in the doll's house, of the effects of a lack of education and experience which might provide them with alternative spheres in which to assert their independence; of sexual repression and the imposition of attempting to uphold an unattainable cultural ideal. Only in this case of those who turn to religion is something of an explanation given. Mrs Clennam gives a fairly full account of herself (but then, unlike Mrs Varden, she has not been presented mockingly) and in *American Notes* a yet more sympathetic analysis of women's enthusiasm for evangelicalism is presented, when it is spoken of as being resorted to 'as a strong drink, and as an escape from the dull monotonous round of home' (AN: 3). But, as Michael Slater has pointed out, when such tendencies are resorted to in the novels, they are almost always shown to be the result either of simple-minded gullibility, or of sheer perversity.[4]

Again, the answer lies in the impossibility of describing these women in terms of 'real' characters, where the author suggests that a process of cause and effect, of growth, development or repression lies behind their psychological and social being. They are, rather, dramatised points taken from a schematic structuring of the notion of womanhood: those who wilfully deny their proper womanly role. Their overt fuction is far more the amusement of the reader than the teaching of any specific moral lesson: their long-term effect, however, is to reinforce and perpetuate both stereotypes and the type of humour which they feed.

Similar perversion of womanhood is found in Dickens' portrayals of campaigning women. Here, because there is a clearer ideological didacticism at work on Dickens' part, his satirical victims more easily trigger off our anger. Not that there is anything new in this response. John Stuart Mill wrote to his wife in 1865 that

> That creature Dickens, whose last story, Bleak House, I found accidentally at the London Library the other day & took home & read—much the worst of his things, & the only one of them I altogether dislike—has the vulgar impudence in this thing to ridicule the rights of women. It is done too in the very vulgarest way—just the stile in which vulgar men used to ridicule 'learned ladies' as neglecting their children & household &c.[5]

Bleak House does, certainly, contain some of Dickens' most conspicuous agitating women: Mrs Jellyby, her eyes fixed on the natives in Borrioboola Gha rather than on her child stuck between the area railings or on the dish of potatoes which has become mislaid in the coal bucket, and last glimpsed going in for 'the rights of women to sit in Parliament' (BH: 67); Mrs Pardiggle, requisitioning her children's pocket-money for the Tockahoopo Indians and the Infant Bonds of Joy; and Miss Wisk, who attends Caddy Jellyby's wedding indignantly proclaiming that 'the idea of woman's mission lying chiefly in the narrow sphere of Home was an outrageous slander on the part of her Tyrant, Man' (BH: 30). Dickens was, of course, rehearsing topical satire. 'Bloomerism' had come to England in 1851: *Punch* cartoons, in the early part of the year, began by poking fun at the idea of women in trousers; and finished it by a concerted attack on women invading a range .of traditionally male occupations. Dickens himself joined in the assault against the fashion and the characteristics of its adherents in his *Household Words* article 'Sucking Pigs'.[6] Mrs Bellows is his unsubtle handle for those who

> must agitate, agitate, agitate. She must take to the little table and water-bottle. She must go in to be a public character. She must work right away at a Mission. It is not enough to do right for right's sake. There can be no satisfaction for Mrs Bellows, in satisfying her mind after due reflection that what she contemplates is right, and therefore ought to be done, and so in calmly and quietly doing it, conscious that therein she sets a righteous example which never can in the nature of things be lost and thrown away. Mrs Bellows has no business to be self-dependent, and to preserve a quiet little avenue of her own in the world, begirt with her own influences and duties.[7]

In other words, she, just like Mrs Jellyby, is in complete contrast to Esther.

It was not that Dickens was unaware, in a limited sense, of the problems facing certain women in society. In 1842, he wrote to the *Morning Chronicle* strongly supporting Lord Ashley's Bill prohibiting the employment of women in the mines, although he ignored the fact that such employment was, for many, an economic necessity. In *Nicholas Nickleby*, as well as *The Chimes*, he attacked the exploitation of those working in the clothing trade: 'many sickly girls, whose business, like that of the poor worm, is to produce, with patient toil, the finery that bedecks the thoughtless and luxurious' (NN: 17). As Richard Altick has reminded us, even without the hints offered by the ogling Mr Mantalini, this employment would have carried particular overtones for many readers:

> For it was well known that girls like her were exposed to the wiles of men both inside the shop and on the pavement outside as well. By the mere deed of enrolling Kate in the dressmaking trade, therefore, Dickens was able to arouse in his readers a concern which he did not need to make explicit ... laying the groundwork for the later development in which the danger of seduction was made explicit, Kate's becoming the prey of Lord Frederick Verisopht and Sir Mulberry Hawk.[8]

Dickens made the Governesses' Benevolent Institution an exception to his habitual declining of invitations to speak at charity functions, since 'their cause has my warmest sympathy';[9] he gave both moral and active support to Angela Burdett-Coutts in her Urania Cottage project, which offered accommodation and assistance to prostitutes wishing to give up their trade and, subsequently, to young women in danger of turning to prostitution through necessity. But the substance of the 'Appeal to Fallen Women' which he addressed to the potential inmates of the refuge is telling. He claimed that Miss Coutts aimed 'to make a HOME for them. In this Home they will be taught all household work that would be useful to them in a home of their own and enable them to make it comfortable and happy.[10] Eventually, after emigration, they may—like Martha in *David Copperfield*— 'become the faithful wives of honest men, and live and die in peace'.[11] Emigration, of course, was also a favourite solution for a further contemporary 'problem': that of the 405,000 'surplus women' revealed in the 1861 census, for whom statistically there was no husband. Yet Dickens does not consider, explicitly, this possible impediment to a woman taking up her position at the centre of that proper sphere of action, the home. For, unlike those Exeter Hall Jellyby types, trying to make 'the last great outer circle first', the ideal, rather, is that which Esther hesitantly put forward to Mrs Pardiggle: 'I thought it best to be as useful as I could, and to render what kind services I could, to those immediately about me; and to try to let that circle of duty gradually and naturally expand itself' (BH: 8). In many ways, in Dickens' terms, women were in a fortunate position, knowing from where they should begin their assault on the muddle which is society. For the appearance of unity which can be given by the concepts of marriage and home, however illusory in fact, is, of course, a highly convenient fictional device. As we have already seen, it provides a neat rounding-off point for certain strands of the narrative. Moreover, marriage would, on the surface, seem to be one clear area in which Dickens could organise relations within society by reference to a 'natural' order and system.

But within Dickens' texts two things work to disrupt and subvert this organisation: the first is the question of women's sexuality; the second is the power wielded by the presence of those women who fail to be contained by the polarities of brides and gorgons. Although Miss Wade or Edith Dombey, for example, do not occupy the centre of their respective novels, the very irregularity of their presence serves to question the stability of that centre.

In writing about sexuality, two major difficulties faced Dickens: the issue of literary propriety, with the publishers and libraries which served family reading anxious to distribute nothing which might 'bring a blush into the cheek of the young person' (OMF: I,11); and the fact that, even excluding questions of propriety and admissibility, there was no clear agreement as to what constituted the 'natural' in the area of female sexuality. On the one hand, there were the voices which denied it, which could be found both in socio-moralistic works, and in medical reference texts. W.R. Greg, writing of prostitution in *The Great Sin of Great Cities*, informed his readers that: 'in men ... the sexual desire is inherent and spontaneous. In the other sex, the desire is dormant, if not non-existent'.[12] Even later on in the nineteenth century, Acton's authoritative *The Functions and Disorders of the Reproductive Organs* took a half-way position: one could tell *respectable* English wives and mothers since they were incapable of such sensations: 'Love of home, children and domestic duties, are the only passion they feel.'[13] Yet there were other opinions on the matter. A correspondent wrote to *The Times* in 1847, for example, complaining that:

> One would really think, to listen to some sentimentalists, that man alone derived any sensual gratification from these indulgences, and that there were no animal passions in woman to tempt her in the same direction. Women yield, not to the solicitation of men, but to the solicitations of their own impure desire. . .[14]

Dickens' texts seem to embody both pessimistic possibilities: sexlessness, and the existence of a sexuality which is damaging and dangerous to both woman and man, as well as acknowledging, often in a coyly covert way, the sexual attraction which women can hold for men.

On the one hand, some of those who 'fall', like Nancy in *Oliver Twist*, seem propelled to this fate by economic necessity and social circumstance. On the other hand, although it is never made explicit, there is a suggestion that Steerforth, for example, exploits less controllable forces in

Em'ly than a desire to better her social position. The acme of spiritual and domestic perfection, Agnes, gives off so negligible an aura of sexual materiality that George Orwell could gibe that she was the 'real legless angel of Victorian romance'.[15] But in general, those women who appear in the novels as the most obvious candidates for marriage are not denied physicality. Yet this physicality is habitually manifested in terms which are superficially unthreatening, since it is turned towards taboo objects of desire—fathers, brothers, pets. Bella and her father exchange open caresses in *Our Mutual Friend*: the intimate dinner which they enjoy at Greenwich is described as an 'innocent elopement'. David Copperfield daydreams frantically as Dora holds Jip in her arms, rests her dimpled chin on his head, and calls him 'my pet' (DC: 26). Ruth Pinch, in her and Tom's new rooms in Islington, is seen 'bustling to and fro, busy about a hundred pleasant nothings, stopped every now and then to give old Tom a kiss' (MC: 36). Helena and Neville Landless have a partnership which seems to rest on more passionate energy than that between any married couple: 'half shy, half defiant; fierce of look; an indefinable kind of pause coming and going on their whole expression, both of face and form' (ED: 6).

Repressed incestuous sentiment may or may not be lurking in some of the embraces. Welsh, in *The City in Dickens*, is unwilling to see it as such, wanting to explain the gestures as further examples of the succouring role of women, reinforcing the pleasures of hearth and home.[16] For the physical pampering by daughters invariably takes place when there is a complete family unit. A more responsible loyalty takes over when the daughter is an actual, rather than a symbolic replacement for a wife, as with Agnes Wickfield, or Lizzie Hexham, or Lucie Manette, or Amy Dorrit. It certifies their future aptitude to take on a house of their own. But the behaviour of, say, Bella, or Dolly Varden, or Dora, is less clearcut. It suggests the girls' potential ability to deliver the sexual goods, but maintains their innocence in terms of strict literary propriety. However, as we have already seen in the cases of Bella and Dora, sexuality without housewifely responsibility is hardly enough; and Dolly, though not treated on quite so serious a level as these two protagonists, also has her lesson to learn. 'I was so vain and giddy', she admits, safe in the embrace of Joe's remaining arm (BR: 78). Sexuality, in all these cases, is overtly assimilated, controlled, by the demands of a moral-reinforcing plot.

But the sexuality of the women in *Barnaby Rudge*, as elsewhere, serves to disrupt not the ostensible organisation of the fiction, but the relationship between author, reader and the female subject. For the narrator, as well as his male protagonists, ogles his females. Given the physical, rather than emotional terms of reference in which he describes Dolly comforting Emma Haredale, it is hard to postulate a hypothetical woman reader as the addressee. When she 'laid her cheek to hers, and put her arms about her', he asks:

> what mortal eyes could have avoided wandering to the delicate bodice, the streaming hair, the neglected dress, the perfect abandonment and unconsciousness of the blooming little beauty? Who could look on and see her lavish caresses and endearments, and not desire to be in Emma Haredale's place; to be either her or Dolly; either the hugging or the hugged?
> (BR: 59)

This passage, in particular, provokes unease when one looks back to the 'handsome satyr', Hugh, boldly harassing Dolly on her return from The Warren (BR: 21). This previous episode is charged with fear on the girl's part; it helps set up future romantic promise when Joe rescues her. But, as Sylvère Monod has indicated, the fact that this wild man of the woods has the advantage of being uninhibited about his own amorous activities might have been 'a state of things that, at a deep level of Dickens' subconscious, must have appeared as most enviable.'[17]

Barnaby Rudge is not the only novel in which Dickens spectates from a position of vicarious male desire. He develops a tone of coy whimsicality when describing Ruth Pinch, licking his lips over more than the forthcoming steak and kidney pudding, she

> being one of those little women to whom an apron is a most becoming little vanity, it took an immense time to arrange; having to be carefully smoothed down beneath—Oh, heaven, what a wicked little stomacher! and to be gathered up into little plaits by the strings before it could be tied, and to be tapped, rebuked, and wheedled, at the pockets, before it would be set right, which at last it did, and when it did—but never mind; this is a sober chronicle. (MC: 39)

He is an assiduous collector of dimples and ringlets and blushes, of quivering young bodies. 'Why,' he observes of Barbara's response to Kit Nubbles, 'she is trembling now! Foolish, fluttering Barbara!' (OCS: 68). In other words, it is not just the presence, sometimes repressed, often marshalled, of female sexuality within the texts which threatens with potentially disruptive energies. Male desire is strongly present too: not so obvious in the passions which motivate Dickens' heroes and villains (with the probable exception of Bradley Headstone), but in the implicit creation, in terms of point of view, of a particular bond between narrator and male reader. This, in its turn, throws one back to the other women within the fictions, and to the male-organised sexual ideology into which they have been placed. The woman reader, now or then, is forced to insert herself into the texts and take up a position which is not articulated through the apparent author–reader relationship.

One reason why the women with the most power to disrupt

within Dickens' novels can wield this power so effectively is that their words or actions are frequently left uncommented on or unassimilated. Edith Dombey, certainly, ruminates bitterly on her past, on the manner in which her mother has fostered the characteristics of pride and self-contempt within her; but her future, in terms of the plot, is to be cast out, an anomaly, into self-imposed but inevitable exiled limbo in southern Italy with Cousin Feenix. The physically and emotionally scarred Rosa Dartle, is left stamping her foot and flashing her eyes, a perpetual emblem of falsely-based class hatred and of more justified sexual betrayal. Estella, throughout *Great Expectations*, is both manipulated and manipulator: the means through which Miss Havisham hopes to revenge *her* betrayal by a man, and a taunter of Pip on both class and emotional grounds. That she makes, initially, an unhappy marriage is clear, as is the fact, in the original ending of the novel, that there is little hint of her expiating her faults through this: she is left riding away in her carriage conveying the fact that she has passed through a period of sombre suffering. In the revised version, her destiny is as uncertain as that of Pip, seeing 'no shadow of a future parting'. If that shadow is one last example of Pip's lack of foresight and self-knowledge, it can become, for the reader, a premonition of one further capricious act on Estella's part. The effect on the reader is to make Estella, at the end, as unpredictable to us as she has been to Pip throughout the book. For we have continually been denied access to her own voice, her own point of view. The first-person narrative has, again, ensured this.

Perhaps even more disturbing are the occasional women who make brief, unannounced, unpursued appearances, as with Little Dorrit and Maggy's dawn encounter with a suicidal female near London Bridge, or the woman at the races in a handsome carriage, accompanied by two men, to whom Nell offers a nosegay, 'and taking her flowers put money into her trembling hand, and bade her go home and keep at home for God's sake' (OCS: 19). She is the one character in the novel with the realism to percieve that Nell, an adolescent girl wandering the country with an enfeebled grandfather, is in distinct sexual danger. Different again is Estella's mother, who, in a novel which openly stresses the emotional force which bitter and repressed women can turn in on themselves and on the lives of others, reminds us of a different type of force as her employer demands that she shows off her strong scarred wrists.

The most disquieting of all these examples is Miss Wade in *Little Dorrit*. She neither plays a central part in the plot construction, nor serves to reinforce the callousness of another character (as Rosa Dartle is a masochistic foil to Steerforth), nor emerges to give an isolated jolt to the reader's sense of a sexually ordered world. Certainly, she provides one of the novel's repeated images of imprisonment, a 'self-tormentor' caught, like some of the other examples, within her own past, and her own pride and feeling of superiority. Yet to a reader today, if not perhaps in 1857, she seems trapped in her own sexuality. The passion she felt for her schoolfriend is voiced far more strongly than her love for her fiancé (in which her aggrieved sense of her social position predominates) or her strange attachment to Gowan. The girlfriend 'tormented my love beyond endurance'; would deliberately 'drive me wild with jealousy'. Holding her in her arms after one of their sessions of mutual accusation, she would spend the night

> loving her as much as ever, and often feeling as if, rather than suffer so, I could so hold her in my arms and plunge to the bottom of a river—where I would still hold her after we were both dead. (LD: II,21)

Her enticing away of Tattycoram has an overtly social

131

purpose—to rescue the orphan girl from the ignominy which the well-meaning, but emotionally obtuse Meagles had imposed upon her from the very moment they christened her with that demeaning nickname. It is an understandable motive on the part of Miss Wade, which is rendered somewhat problematical in the long run by the humbly subservient, and apparently non-satiric manner in which Tattycoram is ultimately seen returning to her proxy family. At least the Meagles represent a mode of exploitation which she, and the reader, understand. For the way Miss Wade is described leading Tattycoram away from the Meagles, arm round her waist, her stance 'suggesting to an observer, with extraordinary force, in her composure itself (as a veil will suggest the form it covers), the unquenchable passion of her own nature' (LD: I,27) combines with the description of the effect she has on the young girl—'Her rich colour, her quick blood, her rapid breath'. These are all normal terms of approval from Dickens for a heroine in an attractive state of emotional agitation and hence have unmistakable overtones of Miss Wade's sexual power.

We cannot reconstruct whether or not the full implications would have been clear to either Dickens or the nineteenth-century reader. As Pearsall states, in his discussion of lesbianism:

> If the man in the street was oblivious to homosexuality in men, how much more was he so in respect of homosexuality in women ... female homosexuality was the love that could not speak its name simply because the state was undefined.[18]

In any case, literary convention would have precluded the articulation rather than the suggestion of this (or, for that matter, David's relationship with Steerforth), just as they did with heterosexual matters. But the presence of Miss Wade,

who combines a particular brand of sexual power with
vehement anger at forms of class domination, acts, like the
presence of all the women whose unmarried status in one way
or another ensures their marginalisation within Dickens' texts,
as a strong reminder of the potentially unstable grounds on
which Dickens' desired norm is founded. He appeals to the
natural, to the God-given: 'every home in all this land' is 'a
World, in which a woman's course of influence and action is
marked out by Heaven!'[19] But in fact, the desideratum defines
itself, within the texts, as the elimination of all those forces
which threaten to disrupt it. Among those forces can be seen
the desire of women to determine the sphere of their own
lives, and to see themselves through their own eyes. This
latter demand is precisely the challenge which a feminist
reading throws out to Dickens' texts.

The application of feminist criticism provides us with a
strategy of reading which is in direct contrast to the
viewpoints held by Dickens and written, explicitly and
implicitly, into his texts. It demands a blending of the
synchronic and diachronic readings outlined earlier in this
study, and, by inserting the factor of sexual difference,
highlights once more the degree to which irresolvable
contradiction, of all types, permeates Dickens' writing. Like
the other strategies which have been offered, it provides no
easy answers but, like all worthwhile types of criticism, it
offers us a further means of asking questions about Dickens'
novels. It is only through the posing of questions, and
through a willingness to accept the fact that the responses
thrown up may be both difficult and inconsistent, that we can
come to learn more about Dickens' methods of composition,
about the relationship of his work to its time, and about our
own methods of reading.

Notes

Chapter 1

1. John Forster, *The Life of Charles Dickens*, ed. J.W.T. Ley (London, 1928), p. 35.
2. Ibid., p. 29.
3. F.S. Schwarzbach, *Dickens and the City* (London, 1978), p. 17.
4. Forster, *Life*, p. 818.
5. John Butt and Kathleen Tillotson, *Dickens at Work* (London, 1957), p. 66, quoting William Jerdan, *Autobiography* (London 1852), IV, p. 364.
6. Forster, *Life*, p. 473.
7. Butt and Tillotson, *Dickens at Work*, p. 109.
8. Charles Dickens, *The Letters of Charles Dickens*, ed. Walter Dexter (London, 1938), II, p. 272.
9. Forster, *Life*, p. 346.
10. Quoted in Gladys Storey, *Dickens and Daughter* (London, 1939), p. 92.
11. Edward Bulwer Lytton, *England and the English* (London, 1833, II, p.165).
12. William Wordsworth, *The Prelude* (1805 edn), VII, 11, 595–8.
13. Frederick Engels, *The Condition of the Working Class in England*

(Leipzig, 1845), translated by Florence Kelly-Wischnewetzky; Karl Marx and Frederick Engels, *Collected Works*, 4 (London, 1975), pp. 328–9.

14. Benjamin Disraeli, *Sybil* (London, 1845; Bradenham edn, London, 1927), IX, p. 77.
15. Quoted in Steven Marcus, *Dickens: from Pickwick to Dombey* (London, 1965), p. 61.
16. Unsigned review [? G.H. Lewes], *National Magazine and Monthly Critic*, i, 1837, pp. 445–6.
17. Richard D. Altick, *The English Common Reader* (Chicago and London, 1957), pp. 383–4. Popular though Dickens was, he was clearly outsold by, for example, G.W.M. Reynolds' penny romances.
18. This opinion was voiced by a local speaker at a presentation and banquet in Dickens' honour, 4 December 1858: *The Speeches of Charles Dickens*, ed. K.J. Fielding (Oxford, 1960), p. 286.
19. Walter Besant, *Fifty Years Ago* (London, 1888), pp. 2–3.
20. William Makepeace Thackeray, 'De Juventute', *Roundabout Papers* (London, 1863), ed. George Saintsbury (London, 1908), p. 424. The article first appeared in the *Cornhill Magazine*, October 1860.
21. Quoted by Marcus, *Dickens*, p. 45.
22. 'The Niger Expedition', *Examiner*, 19 August 1848, reprinted in Dickens, *Collected Papers*, I (London, 1937), pp. 176–7.
23. *The Crystal Palace, and its Contents; being an illustrated cyclopaedia of the Industry of All Nations* (London, 1852), p. 282.
24. Dickens, *Speeches*, p. 128.
25. Ibid., pp. 128–9.
26. John Ruskin, 'The Eagle's Nest', Lecture II, *The Works of John Ruskin*, ed. E.T. Cook and Alexander Wedderburn (London, 1903–12), XXII, pp. 147–8.
27. Unsigned review [George Brimely], 'Dickens's Bleak House', *Spectator*, 26, 24 September 1853, p. 924.

Chapter 2

1. Charles Dickens, *Miscellaneous Papers*, ed. B.W. Matz (London, 1908), p. 40.
2. For a full exposition of this type of reading, see Pierre

Macherey, *A Theory of Literary Production* (Paris, 1966), translated by Geoffrey Wall (London, 1978), pp. 3–101; and Terry Eagleton, *Criticism and Ideology* (London, 1976), pp. 89–101.

3. Robert Weimann, 'Past Significance and Present Meaning in Literary History', *Structure and Society in Literary History* (London, 1977), pp. 18–56.

4. See, for example, 'The Detective Police', 'Three "Detective" Anecdotes' and 'On Duty with Inspector Field', in Charles Dickens, *Reprinted Pieces* (London, 1858).

5. Quoted by Hesketh Pearson, *Oscar Wilde* (New York, 1946), p. 208.

6. Aldous Huxley, *Vulgarity in Literature* (London, 1930), p. 54.

7. Fitzjames Stephen, *Cambridge Essays* (London, 1855), pp. 174 n., 175.

8. For consideration of the changing critical response to the death of Little Nell, see George H. Ford, *Dickens and his Readers* (Princeton, 1955), pp. 55–71; and Dennis Walder, *Dickens and Religion* (London, 1981), pp. 66–90.

9. Edgar Johnson, *Charles Dickens. His Tragedy and Triumph* (London, 1953), pp. 325–9.

10. Schwarzbach, *Dickens and the City*, pp. 70–5.

11. Dickens, *Letters*, ed. Walter Dexter, II, p. 695.

12. Susan R. Horton, *The Reader in the Dickens World* (London, 1981), p. 7.

13. Dickens, *Speeches*, p. 19.

14. Ibid., p. 24.

15. Ibid., p. 29.

16. Dickens, *Letters*, ed. Walter Dexter, II, p. 546.

17. Ibid.

18. For a further discussion of this passage from 'Meditations in Monmouth Street' and its implications for a discussion of Dickens and realism, see J. Hillis Miller, 'The Fiction of Realism: *Sketches by Boz, Oliver Twist*, and Cruikshank's Illustrations', *Dickens Contennial Essays*, ed. Ada Nisbet and Blake Nevius (London, 1971), pp. 85–153.

Chapter 3

1. Mikhail Bakhtin, *Problems of Dostoevsky's Poetics*, edited and

translated by Caryl Emerson (Manchester, 1984), p. 6.

2. Jacques Derrida, 'Structure, Sign and Play in the Discourse of the Human Sciences', *The Languages of Criticism and the Sciences of Man*, ed. Richard Macksey and Eugenio Donato (Baltimore, 1970), p. 248.

3. Steven Marcus, 'Human Nature, Social Orders, and 19th-Century Systems of Explanation: Starting In with George Eliot', *Salmagundi*, 28 (1975), p. 25.

4. Quoted by Michael Slater, *Dickens and Women* (London, 1983), p. 255.

5. *Spectator*, 24 September 1853, p. 923.

6. The attraction of the underworld has proved exceptionally strong for some readers. James R. Kincaid admits that the text is a clearly didactic story, but turns the expected interpretation on its head: it bears the moral: 'virtue stinks. Against Oliver's triumph over the thieves is played the subversive story of the triumph of the thieves' lively and fiercely justified style over the dead world (joined by Oliver) of what used to be called the establishment' (James R. Kincaid, 'Coherent Readers, Incoherent Texts', *Critical Inquiry*, 3 (1977), p. 789). Terry Eagleton, in *Criticism and Ideology*, makes a similar point with greater subtlety. For him, the novel argues that Oliver both *is* and *is not* the product of bourgeois oppression: 'just as the "real" world of bourgeois social relations into which he is marginally rescued is enclosed against the "unreal" underworld of poverty and crime, while simultaneously being shown up by that underworld as illusory.'

7. Humphry House, *The Dickens World* (London, 1941), p. 169.

8. Fr. F.X. Shea, 'Mr. Venus Observed: The Plot Change in *Our Mutual Friend*', *Papers on Language and Literature*, IV (1968), pp. 170–81.

9. Stanley Friedman, 'The Motif of Reading in *Our Mutual Friend*', *Nineteenth-Century Fiction*, 28 (1973), p. 52.

10. Victor Sklovskij, 'The Mystery Novel: Dickens' *Little Dorrit*', *Readings in Russian Poetics*, ed. Ladislav Matejka and Krystyna Pomorska (Cambridge, Mass. and London, 1971), pp. 220–6.

11. Seymour Chatman, *Story and Discourse* (London, 1978), p. 19.

12. Kate Perugini, '"Edwin Drood", and the Last Days of Charles Dickens', *Pall Mall Magazine*, June 1906, p. 644; emphasis added.

Chapter 4

1. Barbara Hardy, *The Appropriate Form* (London, 1970), pp. 7–8.
2. Raymond Williams, *The Country and the City* (London, 1973), p. 154.
3. Ibid., p. 155.
4. Raymond Williams discusses this passage from *Dombey and Son* in his introduction to the Penguin edition of the novel (London, 1970). Peter K. Garret, in *The Victorian Multiplot Novel: Studies in Dialogical Form* (London, 1980), also has some very interesting points to make about the figure of Asmodeus, on which I have drawn in this chapter.
5. E.M. Forster, *Aspects of the Novel* (London, 1927), p. 98.
6. Roland Barthes, 'Introduction to the Structural Analysis of Narratives', *Image–Music–Text*, Essays selected and translated by Stephen Heath (London, 1977), pp. 104–7. In this section, Barthes makes use of A.J. Greimas, *Cours de sémantique structurale* (Paris, 1964).
7. Ibid., p. 111.
9. Jonathan Arac, *Commissioned Spirits* (New Brunswick, 1979), p. 51
9. K.J. Fielding and A.W. Brice, 'Bleak House and the Graveyard', *Dickens the Craftsman*, ed. Robert B. Partlow, Jr (Carbondale, 1970), pp. 115–39.
10. Walder, *Dickens and Religion*, p. 158.
11. George Eliot, 'The Natural History of German Life', *Essays of George Eliot*, ed. Thomas Pinney (London, 1963), p. 270, reprinted from *Westminster Review*, LXVI (1856), pp. 51–79.
12. Michel Foucault, *Discipline and Punish* (Paris, 1976), translated by Alan Sheridan (London, 1977), p. 201.
13. Forster, *Life*, p. 721.
14. For an extended treatment of this issue, see H. Daleski, *Dickens and the Art of Analogy* (London, 1970).
15. See further Philip Collins, '*Little Dorrit*: the Prison and the Critics', *Times Literary Supplement*, 18 April 1980, pp. 445–6.
16. Forster, *Life*, p. 650.
17. Horton, *The Reader in the Dickens World*, p. 87.
18. Unsigned article [Charles Dickens], 'Nobody, Somebody, and Everybody', *Household Words*, 30 August 1856, p. 146.
19. Karl Marx and Frederick Engels, *The Communist Manifesto*

(1848), translated by Samuel Moore (1888), Penguin edition (London, 1967), p. 82.

Chapter 5

1. Forster, *Life*, p. 39.
2. Ibid., p. 347.
3. Ruskin, letter to Charles Eliot Norton, 19 June 1870, *Works*, XXXVII, p. 7.
4. Unsigned article [Charles Dickens], 'The Noble Savage', *Household Words*, VII, 11 June 1853, p. 337.
5. Thomas Carlyle, *The French Revolution* (London, 1837), Book I, Chapter II (London, 1896), i, p. 14.
6. Forster, *Life*, p. 560.
7. See Robert F. Wearmouth, *Methodism and the Working-Class Movements of England, 1800–1850* (London, 1937).
8. Marcus, *Dickens*, p. 172.
9. *The Life and Struggles of William Lovett* (London, 1876), p. 209 ff., quoted by Marcus, *Dickens*, p. 181.
10. Charlotte Brontë, *Shirley* (London, 1849), Penguin edition, ed. Andrew and Judith Hook (London, 1974), p. 335.
11. Dickens, *Miscellaneous Papers*, p. 133.
12. Raymond Williams, 'The Reader in *Hard Times*', *Writing in Society* (London, [1984]), p. 170.
13. Ibid., p. 171.
14. Harriet Beecher Stowe, *Sunny Memories of Foreign Lands* (London, 1854), p. 185.
15. Unsigned article [Margaret Oliphant], 'Sensation Novels', *Blackwood's Edinburgh Magazine*, 91 (1862), p. 574.
16. See *Letters from Charles Dickens to Angela Burdett-Coutts 1841–1865*, ed. Edgar Johnson (London, 1953); and K.J. Fielding, 'Dickens' Work with Miss Coutts:—I, Nova Scotia Gardens and What Grew There', *Dickensian*, 61 (1965), pp. 112–19.
17. Unsigned articles [Charles Dickens] in the *Examiner*: 'The Paradise at Tooting', 20 January 1849; 'The Tooting Farm', 27 January 1849; 'The Recorder's Charge', 3 March 1849; 'The Verdict for Drouet', 21 April 1849. See also K.J. Fielding and A.W. Brice, 'Dickens and the Tooting Disaster', *Victorian Studies*, XII, 1968, pp. 227–44.
18. Dickens, *The Letters of Charles Dickens*, Pilgrim edition, ed. Kathleen Tillotson, IV (London, 1977), p. 566.

19. Forster, *Life*, p. 347.
20. Ruskin, 'The Two Paths' (1859), *Works*, XVI, pp. 337–8.
21. D.H. Lawrence, 'Nottingham and the Mining Country', *Phoenix*, ed. Edward D. McDonald (London, 1936), p. 140.
22. Dickens, *Speeches*, p. 340.
23. Ibid., p. 50.
24. Dickens, 'Wallotty Trot', *Household Words*, VI, 5 February 1853, p. 501.
25. Ruskin, letter to Charles Eliot Norton, 19 June 1870, *Works*, XXXVII, p. 7.
26. Dickens, *Letters*, Pilgrim edition, I (London, 1965), ed. Madeline House and Graham Storey, pp. 483–4.
27. See Patrick Brantlinger, 'Dickens and the Factories', *Nineteenth-Century Fiction*, 26 (1971), p. 275.
28. Philip Collins, 'Dickens and Industrialism', *Studies in English Literature*, 20 (1980), pp. 651–73.
29. Dickens, *Letters*, Pilgrim edition, ed. Madeline House and Graham Storey (London, 1965), p. 447.
30. Quoted ibid., IV ed. Tillotson, p. 211, fn. 1.
31. Ibid.
32. Quoted in Michael Slater, 'Dickens' Tract for the Times', *Dickens 1970*, ed. Michael Slater, (London, 1970), p. 106.
33. Sheila M. Smith, 'John Overs to Charles Dickens: A Working-Man's Letter and its Implications', *Victorian Studies*, XVIII (1974), pp. 195–217.
34. Unsigned article [Henry Morley], 'Ground in the Mill', *Household Words*, 22 April 1854, p. 224.
35. Quoted in the Norton Critical Edition of *Hard Times*, ed. George Ford and Sylvère Monod (New York, 1966), p. 252.
36. Unsigned article [Charles Dickens], 'The Noble Savage', *Household Words*, 11 June 1853, p. 337.
37. Unsigned article [Charles Dickens], 'On Strike', Ibid., 11 February 1854, pp. 553–9. See also Geoffrey Carnall, 'Dickens, Mrs Gaskell and the Preston Strike', *Victorian Studies*, VIII (1964), pp. 31–48; and David Lodge, 'The Rhetoric of Hard Times', *Language of Fiction*, (London, 1966), pp. 144–63, as well as Williams, 'The Reader in *Hard Times*'.

Chapter 6

1. Coventry Patmore, 'The Angel in the House', Book I, Canto

IV, 'The Morning Call: Preludes I. The Rose of the World', ll. 11–12; and Book II, Canto II, 'The Course of the Love: Preludes I. The Changed Allegiance', ll. 94–5.

2. Ruskin, 'Sesame and Lilies', *Works*, XVIII, p. 122.
3. The idea that the modern family is *not* a vestigial unit struggling against the demands of industrialisation and individualism, but is a product of it, has been strongly put in Philippe Ariès, *Centuries of Childhood: a social history of family life*, translated by Robert Baldick (New York, 1962); Mark Spilka, *Dickens and Kafka* (London, 1963); and Alexander Welsh, *The City of Dickens* (Oxford, 1971).
4. Slater, *Dickens and Women*, p. 228.
5. John Stuart Mill, *The Later Letters of John Stuart Mill 1849–1873*, I (London, 1972), ed. Francis E. Mineka and Dwight N. Lindley, p. 190.
9. Unsigned article [Charles Dickens], 'Sucking Pigs', *Household Words*, 8 November 1851, pp. 145–7.
7. Ibid., p. 146.
8. Richard Altick, 'Victorian Readers and the Sense of the Present', *Midway*, 11 (1970), pp. 100–1.
9. Dickens, *Letters*, Pilgrim edition, IV, p. 38.
10. Charles Dickens, 'An Appeal to Fallen Women' (1847), reprinted in *Collected Papers* (London, 1937), p. 80.
11. Ibid., p. 81.
12. Unsigned article [W.R. Greg], 'Prostitution', *Westminster Review*, 53 (1850), p. 456. Reprinted as *The Great Sin of Great Cities* (1853).
13. Dr William Acton, *The Functions and Disorders of the Reproductive Organs, in Childhood, Adult Age, and Advanced Life, Considered in Their Physiological, Social, and Moral Relations* (London, 4th edn, 1865), p. 113.
14. *The Times*, 4 November 1847, p. 6.
15. George Orwell, 'Charles Dickens', *The Collected Essays, Journalism and Letters of George Orwell*, ed. Sonia Orwell and Ian Angus, I, *An Age Like This*, (London, 1968), p. 459.
16. Welsh, *The City of Dickens*, pp. 154–6.
17. Sylvère Monod, 'Rebel With a Cause: Hugh of the Maypole', *Dickens Studies*, I, 1965, pp. 20–21.
18. Ronald Pearsall, *The Worm in the Bud* (London, 1969), p. 475.
19. Dickens, *Letters*, Pilgrim edition, ed. Graham Storey and K.J. Fielding, V (London, 1981), p. 542.

Dickens: A Chronology

1812:   7 February: Charles Dickens born in Portsmouth
1814:   Dickens family moved to London
1817:   Dickens family moved to Chatham, Kent
1822:   Dickens family moved back to Camden Town, London
1824:   Worked in Warren's Blacking Warehouse, for four or five months. His father, John Dickens, imprisoned for four months in the Marshalsea Prison, for debt
1824–27:   Attended the Wellington House Academy, Hampstead Road
1827:   Left school: worked for two firms of solicitors in Gray's Inn
1828:   Became freelance shorthand reporter at Doctors' Commons
1832:   Worked as shorthand reporter for the *Mirror of Parliament* (transcript of parliamentary proceedings) and, for three months, as reporter on new evening paper, the *True Sun*
1833:   Began writing short fictional pieces about London life

1834: Became parliamentary reporter for *Morning Chronicle*, covering political meetings and elections around the country during parliamentary recessions. Under pseudonym 'Boz', published sketches in the *Morning Chronicle* and elsewhere

1835: Began to contribute sketches to the *Evening Chronicle*, edited by George Hogarth. Became engaged to Hogarth's dauther Catherine

1836: *Sketches of Boz* published. In February, invited by William Hall to write text to accompany series of plates by Robin Seymour, illustrating adventures of Nimrod Club. Suggested that the text should precede the pictures: began work on *Pickwick Papers*

31 March: appearance of first number of *Pickwick Papers*: published in volume form 1837

2 April: married Catherine Hogarth

November: became editor of new magazine, *Bentley's Miscellany*: resigned from *Morning Chronicle*

December: *Sketches by Boz* (second series) published

1837: February: *Oliver Twist* began serialisation in *Bentley's Miscellany*: published in volume form 1838

1838: April: first number of *Nicholas Nickleby* appeared: published in volume form 1839

1839: February: gave up editorship of *Bentley's Miscellany*

1840: April: first number of Dickens' weekly magazine, *Master Humphrey's Clock* appeared, with the first episode of *The Old Curiosity Shop* in the fourth number. *Old Curiosity Shop* published in volume form 1841

1841: February: serialisation of *Barnaby Rudge* began in *Master Humphrey's Clock*: published in one volume in December

1842: January–June: in America and Canada, visiting, among other cities, Hartford, New Haven, New

York, Philadelphia, Washington, Baltimore, Pittsburgh, St Louis, Cleveland, Buffalo, Niagara, Toronto, Quebec and Montreal

October: *American Notes* published

1843: January: serialisation of *Martin Chuzzlewit* began: published in volume form 1844

December: *A Christmas Carol* published

1844: July–November: in Italy

December: *The Chimes* published. Returned to Italy

1845: June: returned to England

December: *The Cricket on the Hearth* published

1846: January: became, briefly, editor of the *Daily News*, and, after his resignation the next month, continued to contribute occasional pieces

May: *Pictures from Italy* published. Returned to the Continent until March 1847, staying in Lausanne, Geneva and Paris

October: first number of *Dombey and Son* appeared: published in volume form 1848

1848: December: *The Haunted Man* published

1849: Contributed articles for the *Examiner*

May: serialisation of *David Copperfield* began: published in volume form 1850

1850: March: first number of the weekly magazine *Household Words* appeared

1852: March: serialisation of *Bleak House* began: published in volume form 1853

1854: April: serialisation of *Hard Times* began in *Household Words*, published in volume form later the same year

1855: December: serialisation of *Little Dorrit* began: published in volume form 1857

1858: Separated from his wife: published statement in *Household Words* concerning his 'domestic troubles' and denying 'all the lately whispered rumours' i.e. that the actress Ellen Ternan was his mistress

	August–November: the first of his reading tours, during which he gave 83 readings in the provinces, Scotland and Ireland
1859:	April: first issue of *All the Year Round* appeared, containing opening instalment of *A Tale of Two Cities*, published in volume form later that year. Dickens had quarrelled with Bradbury & Evans, publishers of *Household Words*
1860:	December: serialisation of *Great Expectations* began in *All the Year Round*, published in volume form, 1861
1864:	May; serialisation of *Our Mutual Friend* began: published in volume form 1865
1867:	December–April 1868: reading tour of America
1868	Farewell reading tour, abandoned when Dickens collapsed with illness April 1869
1870:	April: serialisation of *The Mystery of Edwin Drood* began, published (incomplete) September 1870
	9 June: Charles Dickens died

Bibliography

Place of publication is London, unless otherwise stated.

A. *Biographical.*

John Forster, *The Life of Charles Dickens* (1872–74), 1928
  edn, edited by J.W.T. Ley. The most authoritative
  biography of Dickens.
Edgar Johnson, *Dickens: his tragedy and triumph* (1952).
  Thorough in his biographical detail; somewhat speculative
  in points of interpretation.
The Letters of Charles Dickens, Pilgrim (Oxford University
  Press) edition, edited by Kathleen Tillotson. The complete
  letters—currently up to 1838 (vol. V). (1965–81).
  Supplanting the Nonesuch edition of the Letters (3 vols,
  edited Walter Dexter, 1938), which, in any case, are hard
  to get hold of.
The Speeches of Charles Dickens, edited K.J. Fielding,
  (Oxford, 1960). Interesting from the point of view of
  Dickens' public proclamations on a variety of subjects,
  and showing, too, the degree to which he was involved
  with a variety of organisations and institutions.

B. Collections of critical material

Philip Collins, *Charles Dickens: The Critical Heritage* (1971).
John Gross and Gabriel Pearson, *Dickens and the Twentieth Century* (1962).
Ada Nisbet and Blake Nevius, *Dickens Centennial Essays* (1971).
Michael Slater, *Dickens 1970* (1970).
Stephen Wall, *Charles Dickens*, Penguin Critical Anthologies (1970).

C. General critical studies, and works containing important sections on Dickens' writing

Jonathan Arac, *Commissioned Spirits* (New Brunswick, 1979).
John Butt and Kathleen Tillotson, *Dickens at Work* (1957).
John Carey, *The Violent Effigy: A Study of Dickens' Imagination* (1973).
Philip Collins, *Dickens and Crime* (1962).
Philip Collins, *Dickens and Education* (1963).
George H. Ford, *Dickens and his Readers* (Princeton, 1955).
Robert Garis, *The Dickens Theatre* (Oxford, 1965).
Peter K. Garrett, *The Victorian Multiplot Novel: Studies in Dialogical Form* (New Haven, 1980).
Barbara Hardy, *The Moral Art of Charles Dickens* (1970).
John Harvey, *Victorian Novelists and their Illustrators* (1970).
Susan R. Horton, *The Reader in the Dickens World* (1981).
Humphry House, *The Dickens World* (1941).
John Lucas, *The Melancholy Man: A Study of Dickens' Novels* (1970).
Steven Marcus, *Dickens: From Pickwick to Dombey* (1965).
J. Hillis Miller, *Charles Dickens: The World of his Novels* (Cambridge, Mass. 1958).
J. Hillis Miller, *The Form of Victorian Fiction* (Notre Dame, 1968).
Sylvere Monod, *Dickens the Novelist,* (Norman, 1968).

George Orwell, 'Charles Dickens', *Inside the Whale* (1940).

F.S. Schwarzbach, *Dickens and the City* (1979).

Michael Slater, *Dickens and Women* (1983).

Grahame Smith, *Dickens, Money and Society* (Berkeley, 1968).

Sheila M. Smith, *The Other Nation* (Oxford, 1980).

Taylor Stoehr, *Dickens: The Dreamer's Stance* (Ithaca, 1965).

Kathleen Tillotson, *Novels of the Eighteen-Forties* (1961).

Dennis Walder, *Dickens and Religion* (1981).

Alexander Welsh, *The City of Dickens* (Oxford, 1971).

Raymond Williams, *The English Novel from Dickens to Lawrence* (1970).

Raymond Williams, *The Country and the City* (1973).

Edmund Wilson, 'Dickens: The Two Scrooges', *The Wound and the Bow* (1941).

Index

Meagles family (in *Our Mutual Friend*), 65, 77, 132
Meagles, Pet (in *Our Mutual Friend*), 77, 82
Melbourne, Lord, 18
Merdle, Mr (in *Little Dorrit*), 18, 65, 74
metaphor, 28, 29, 37, 44, 65, 74, 77, 108
Metropolitan Commission of Sewers, 74, 75
Metropolitan Sanitary Commissioners: 1848 Report, 44–5
Metropolitan Sanitary Association: First Anniversary Banquet, 1851, 24–5
Micawber family (in *David Copperfield*), 22
Mill, John Stuart, 122
Milton, John, 49
Monod, Sylvère, 128
Morely, Henry; 'Ground in the Mill', 106–7
Morley, John, 22, 23
Morning Chronicle, 45, 59, 123
Morperth, Lord, 96
mortality, child, 40
motherhood, 113
multi-vocal fiction: *see* dialogic fiction
mystery plays, 121
mystery stories, 60–5, 67, 82

Nadgett, Mr (in *Martin Chuzzlewit*), 61
Nancy (in *Oliver Twist*), 47, 60, 126

narrative, complex, 3
narrative, first-person, 48–51, 52, 53–6, 66
narrative theory, 47, 64–7, 72
narrative voice: *see* voice, narrative
narrator, 48–50
National Magazine, 18
Nell (in *The Old Curiosity Shop*), 14, 39–42, 47, 57, 72, 79, 80, 87, 130, 131, 136
Newgate prison, 88, 91
Nickleby, Mrs, 121
Nickleby, Nicholas, 17, 97
Nickleby, Ralph, 61
Nipper, Susan (in *Dombey and Son*), 14
nosalgia, 8
Nova Scotia Gardens, 96
Nubbles family (in *The Old Curiosity Shop*), 79, 117
Nubbles, Kit (in *The Old Curiosity Shop*), 129

Oliphant, Margaret, 95
opening chapters: *see* chapters, opening
Orwell, George, 127
Overs, John, 104
overview: *see* positioning, authorial
Owen, Robert

Pancks (in *Little Dorrit*), 65, 69
panopticon, 76, 78
Pardiggle, Mrs (in *Little Dorrit*), 123, 125
parenthood, 115